The S
LAKES
40 SHORTER WALKS
from the EASY *to*
the ADVENTUROUS

The author and publisher have made every effort to ensure that the information in this publication is accurate, and accept no responsibility whatsoever for any loss, injury or inconvenience experienced by any person or persons whilst using this book.

For India

published by
pocket mountains ltd
The Old Church, Annanside, Moffat, DG10 9HB
pocketmountains.com

ISBN: 978-1-9070250-7-5

A catalogue record for this book is available from the British Library

All route maps are based on 1945 Popular Edition Ordnance Survey material and revised from field surveys by the author © Pocket Mountains Ltd

Printed in Poland

Introduction

The Lake District is England's pre-eminent National Park. Nowhere else is the pattern of mountain, wood and water so compactly and harmoniously arranged. Nowhere else is so comprehensively entwined within a network of paths or cast in raw beauty. As a place to explore on foot it is unique.

This is the second of two books spanning the national park, a companion volume to *The Northern Lakes: 40 Shorter Walks from the Easy to the Adventurous*. Contained within its pages are 40 walks that journey through the landscape and remarkable history of the Southern Lakes, from the Kentmere Valley in the east to the bulk of Black Combe in the west. Along the way, the diverse moods around Ambleside, Grasmere, the Langdales and Coniston are all explored, as are a trio of western valleys – Wasdale, Eskdale and the Duddon Valley.

The Southern Lakes is an area of fascinating nuances and variations. Moving from east to west the tone of the landscape shifts, becoming wilder and less forgiving. More particularly, the extent and manner of human interaction with the landscape changes too. The east is softer and unashamedly touristy, colonised by visitor attractions, car parks and gift shops. Yet, peeking between the trees and over the ridges of the fells, the romance and beauty that first earned the area its reputation survive – pushed to the margins, perhaps, but nonetheless there. Today, of course, the only way to discover those margins is on foot.

Economically, the west resembles the side of the valley thrown into shade. Quieter than the east, more obviously rooted in its agricultural heritage and with shadows of both long past and recently struggling industry at its fringe, it is grittier and less focused upon the visitor. None of this should, however, deter the visitor from making the (probably lengthy) journey there, for this is the Lake District arguably at its most spectacular, most challenging and most rewarding.

About this guide

The ground covered ranges from easy valley strolls to adventurous mountain scrambles, although none of the walks last longer than, at most, half a day. In an area so compact, the emphasis is too often on long days scaling the very highest mountains, or on looping ridges together into extended horseshoes. These are wonderful activities, but they rather overlook the snappy immediacy of many of the Southern Lakes' delights. Here there are ancient woods, nature reserves, mountain tarns, low and mid-height fells, waterfalls, lake shores, sinuous valleys and former quarries to enjoy. These can all be experienced in these digestible walks, which – to extend the metaphor – are more convivial lunches than lengthy feasts. But the 'shorter' in the sub-title does not always mean short (there are serious outings to the Langdale Pikes, Bowfell and Great Gable) – so take it as the relative term it is.

The description of each route begins with the distance to be covered and the height ascended, the relevant Ordnance Survey (OS) 1:25000 map (which should always be carried) and an indication of how long the walk will take. Duration will always be a moot point because of the many variables in play: fit, experienced walkers in spring sunshine will cover the

same ground much more quickly than novices in mist and rain. Timings are intended as a rough guide to assist you in planning your day, and do not allow for any stops you may choose to make. The route map is only a general guide and is emphatically not intended for navigation.

Finally, the contents are arranged east to west, reflecting the fact that the majority of visitors arrive in the national park from the east. This is a journey into the Lakes that explores widely and reaches it glorious conclusion upon the summit of Lingmell.

Getting Around

First, the good news: getting to Windermere, Ambleside and Grasmere by public transport, and moving between them, is a doddle, thanks to the hourly 555 (Lakeslink) bus service between Keswick to the north and Lancaster to the south. Windermere also has the rare luxury of a train service connecting to the West Coast main line at Oxenholme. Between April and October, the length of Great Langdale (up to the Old Dungeon Ghyll Hotel) may be accessed via the excellent 516 (Langdale Rambler) service from Ambleside. Consider seriously the possibility of leaving the car behind – during the school holidays, traffic can be miserable indeed (Ambleside is a notorious bottleneck), with the futile search for somewhere to park an even more glum experience.

South of Skelwith Bridge the scene becomes patchier. The seasonal (April to October) 505 (Coniston Rambler) links Ambleside and Windermere to Hawkshead and Coniston, while the year-round X12 runs north from Ulverston (reached by the X35 from Kendal and Barrow) to Torver and Coniston. See individual walks for which routes are recommended where.

The bad news is that it is next to impossible to access the western valleys without a car. Yes, there is the Cumbrian Coast train line between Barrow and Carlisle and, yes, there is the sketchy X6 bus descending from Whitehaven to Muncaster Castle (and on Sundays to Millom), but these will only get you so far. Wasdale might enjoy a dial-a-taxi service, and Eskdale can call upon the charms of L'al Ratty (steam railway), but there is no escaping the way in which a car opens up these sparsely settled valleys for practical exploration

When committed to the car please exercise caution and consideration: ideally use a recognised car park (the start point usually steers you in that direction anyway); if this is not an option, a small, defined parking area should be. In the rare cases where it is not, be wary of blocking gateways, lanes and passing places. If in doubt, don't – you never know when a much larger vehicle (like a fire engine, say) may need to pass your inappropriately parked car.

Respecting the Environment

The landscape of the Southern Lakes is remarkably resilient. Even so, millions of footsteps each year combined with robust weather systems cause considerable wear and tear – you do not have to look far to see evidence of severely eroded paths. A magnificent volunteer organisation called Fix the Fells (www.fixthefells.co.uk) is fighting back – they have repaired over 100 of the worst paths, with over 70 more in their sights. Please play your part in the process, too: where a footpath exists stick to it, rather

◀ Herdwicks by Burnthwaite, Wasdale Head

than its fringe, walking single file if necessary. Try not to dislodge stones, build pointless cairns (of which there are already many) or cut across zigzags. In the context of the hills these are anti-social activities. Avoid leaving litter at all costs (there is almost nothing more witless and depressing than the sight of stray drinks cans or crisp packets).

More generally, remember the farmers. Use stiles and gates where they exist. Get to grips with the Countryside and Moorland Visitor's Codes. Keep dogs under control, ideally on a lead, especially when close to livestock and farms. Never come between a cow and her calf (with or without a dog). At lambing time, farmers are particularly and understandably sensitive. Remember this is a working landscape – a little respect goes a long way and helps to sustain a harmonious relationship between visitors and locals.

Safety

Do not underestimate the mountains, even if your trip into them is brief, and never underestimate how much more hostile the tops can be than the valleys, even in summer. Sudden weather changes, mist, cold, rain and snow are all part of walking in the Lakes, and while there is certainly a peculiar magic to remote fells in inclement weather, it is a situation best avoided unless properly-equipped. So you will need to have with you, and be confident in using, a map and compass, sometimes in less than ideal circumstances. Decent hillwalking boots are essential, as are waterproofs, warm

◄ Summit cairn, Harter Fell, Eskdale

clothing, food and water. Know your own limitations and be sure to carry the relevant OS 1:25000 map.

A mobile phone is sometimes useful, but cannot be relied on for emergencies – you might not get reception. Always carry a torch, first-aid kit, whistle and watch. Check the weather forecast before you leave and make sure that someone knows where you are going and when you are due to return. Remember that in the end most Mountain Rescue calls are the result of disorientation, slips and exhaustion.

If all this implies that walking in the Southern Lakes is an ordeal to be endured, be assured it is not. Sound preparation, knowledge and equipment, will ensure that your happy expedition remains just that, even when the weather turns, which at some point it will.

Access

The legal 'right to roam', applied locally in May 2005 under the Countryside and Rights of Way Act (2000), opened up new routes to walkers that may previously have been closed off, adding to existing rights of access in the Lake District. Indeed, that right is exercised to a lesser or greater extent in a number of the walks found in this book.

Under the Act, the public has new rights of access on foot to areas classified as open country (mountain, moor, heath and down) and commonland registered for recreational use. The right does not extend to activities such as cycling, canoeing, horse-riding or camping, though existing rights may already be in place for these activities on some land.

There are other restrictions in the Act: for instance, walkers must not damage any wall, fence, hedge, stile or gate in exercising their right of access, and landowners have the right to limit access temporarily.

It is worth familiarising yourself with the legislation and working out what it means for walking in the area. The Ramblers' Association provides more details through its website (www.ramblers.org.uk).

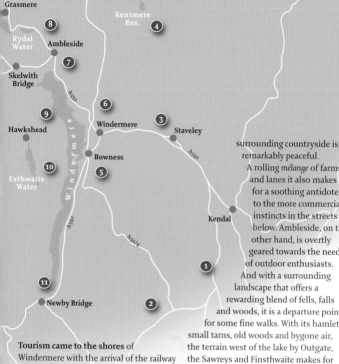

surrounding countryside is remarkably peaceful. A rolling *mélange* of farms and lanes it also makes for a soothing antidote to the more commercial instincts in the streets below. Ambleside, on the other hand, is overtly geared towards the needs of outdoor enthusiasts. And with a surrounding landscape that offers a rewarding blend of fells, falls and woods, it is a departure point for some fine walks. With its hamlets, small tarns, old woods and bygone air, the terrain west of the lake by Outgate, the Sawreys and Finsthwaite makes for explorations as charming and laid back as the landscape itself.

East towards Kendal the country is generally underappreciated, with most visitors happy to zip by on their way to somewhere better known. So seek out the wonderful escarpment at Whitbarrow, the outliers above Staveley and, most of all, the hidden valley of Kentmere. Here, the edge of the majestic Rainsborrow Crag provides a true mountain adventure.

Tourism came to the shores of Windermere with the arrival of the railway in 1847 and never went away. Today, the cluster of towns along the northeast of the lake – Bowness, Windermere and Ambleside – are defined almost as much by tourism as they are by the beauty which first inspired it. If neither Windermere nor Bowness are held in much regard as walking bases (and for most of their visitors the fells are more backdrop than target), the benefit for those prepared to give it a go is that the

8

WINDERMERE, AMBLESIDE AND THE EASTERN APPROACHES

A Sizergh stroll

Distance 5.5km **Time** 1 hour 30
Height gain 13om **Map** OS Explorer OL7
Access there is no direct public transport
to the castle, but the X35 from Barrow to
Kendal stops by the Heaves Hotel,
Levens, a manageable 1km to the south

**With the suggestion of prehistoric
settlement, a splendid castle and the
remains of a deer park, the air around
Sizergh hums with history.**

Start at the National Trust Visitor
Centre, Sizergh Castle (GR497878). Walk
south past the car park entrance, through
a kissing gate into a long pasture sloping
up to the right. Shadow the left-hand wall
into a second field and slant right up the
gentle contours of Sizergh Fell. Entering a
third field, swing left to the prehistoric

cairns and barrow at the crest. Drop a
short way west, enjoying the fine view
across the Lyth Valley to White Scar, then
go through a swing gate and contour
right with the wall to another gate. After
passing through this, descend directly to
and turn right along Parkend Lane, a
recessed, hedgerow-lined minor road.

After 500m, near the tip of the woods of
Brigsteer Park, turn right through a large
estate gate. Immediately branch left
(SP Brigsteer) and rise north through
Flash Bank Deer Park, a broad, tree-fringed
slope above Brigsteer Wood. Gain a grassy
shelf (with flashes of exposed limestone)
and continue up to the edge of the
trees. Veer left, pass through a five-
bar gate, and walk along the scar
top to a vehicular access track.

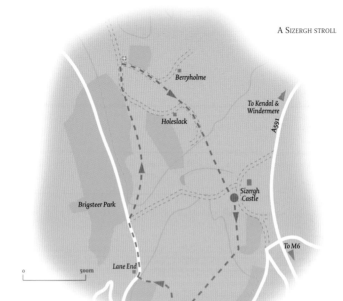

Continue north along the wall-side access track to the weather-beaten but resolute hillside Church of St John, Heslington, where the view west is perhaps at its most sweeping (GR488889).

From the south side of the church take the concrete farm track towards Berryholme. After 350m, as the wall to the right withdraws (by a lone gatepost),

swing right across rough pasture down to a ladder stile, from where you can glimpse the castle through the woods ahead. Press on down to a gate opening to a track. Turn left along the track towards the castle, past a modern farm building and some unsightly pylons. Where the track turns right, continue ahead over a final field back to the visitor centre (1h30).

The Stricklands of Sizergh

The Strickland family first appeared on the scene at Sizergh in 1239, when the land passed, through marriage, to Sir William Strickland. Remarkably, the family still lives in the castle. The core of their home is a 14th-century Peel Tower (one of many built to repel the Scots), with walls 3m-thick in places. With numerous additions and extensions the castle had, by the 18th century, morphed gradually into an impressive fortified mansion, reflecting the considerable wealth and influence of the Stricklands at that time. Since 1950 the castle, its garden and the surrounding 647-hectare estate have been owned by the National Trust.

Windblown on Whitbarrow

**Distance 8.5km Time 2 hours 15
Height gain 220m Map OS Explorer OL7
Access the X35 bus from Barrow-in-Furness
to Kendal stops on the A590 at
Witherslack, 1.5km up the road**

**Vast but intimate, windswept yet
tranquil, capped by a national nature
reserve and ringed by rich woods, the
limestone escarpment of Whitbarrow Scar
is an invigorating place to explore. For
those rushing past on the nearby A590, it
is a case of so near and yet so far . . .**

Start at the crossroads of the old A590
and the road into Mill Side (GR452839),
1.5km east of Witherslack. Walk west on
the road into Mill Side, bearing right after
250m along the farm lane to Low Fell End.
Pass through the farmyard and on to a
short lane that runs up to a gate into
woods. Rise to a track; turn left and
then, 25m on, turn right up a
permissive path. Ascend steeply
to a crafted stone terrace, the

gradient easing as the path slants north.
Just before a bench, cut back to the left by
a marker post and climb to a wall,
hooking around its end and back through
a swing gate. A muddy path leads north
through light woodland which peters out
into sporadic trees and then open fell.

Curve around to the left (NNW) over
firm, limestone-sprinkled ground to gain
a top crowned by a giant cairn and a view
down the length of the scar. A clear path
now dips and rolls broadly NNW over a
series of gentle rounded tops (with more
cairns) to a wall (45 minutes). Over the
stile, weave in the same direction between
blocks of exposed limestone and birch
trees, with a low white escarpment
running to the right. As the escarpment
immediately to the right withdraws,
press on up the gentle slope ahead to

the sturdily-built cairn topping Lord's Seat (GR441871).

A less crafted cairn, just to the west, marks the beginning of a path dropping gradually west for 300m before traversing south into trees. From a stile, descend sharply in tiny zigzags across the face of the scar, then down a steep rake into the valley. Swing left, following the path through a wall stile. Skirt the left edge of a playing field (part of Witherslack Hall, now a school), cross to the next field and then turn sharply right, heading for a gate left of a barn.

Walk through a parking area to the valley road and turn left. (In reverse, there is a great view across to the escarpment, in particular to the bulbous Chapel Head Scar.) After 700m, branch left onto a straight bridleway splitting open pastures and returning to the edge of woodland. Here, the way morphs into a delightful, historic blend of wall and wood, undulating to the road end by Beck Head. The road swoops and curves past scattered cottages (including Beck Head House, with its idyllic, streamside garden) for 750 largely wooded metres to a junction in the 'centre' of Mill Side (with the Mill Pond to the right). Turn left to return to the start point, guided by the roar from the new A590 (2h15).

◀ Limestone escarpment, Whitbarrow

13

Staveley overlook

▲ **Reston Scar** (255m), **Hugill Fell** (273m)

**Distance 3.5km Time 1 hour 15
Height gain 200m Map OS Explorer OL7
Access the hourly 555 from Windermere
to Kendal (and places further afield)
stops in Staveley**

**Tiny outliers like Reston Scar and Hugill
Fell are easy to overlook (and nearly
everyone does), but that would be to
miss one of the most enjoyable short
walks in the eastern approaches.**

Start at the War Memorial, at the
junction of Brow Lane and Church View,
Staveley (GR470985). Walk north along
Church View for 150m until you reach the
weir on the River Kent; branch off to a
lane to the left, then, 20m on, go through
a gate to the left leading into a walled
path. Rise to the stile at its head, joining

a narrow path fenced to the side of a field.
Pass a whitewashed house and turn up
the fellside along a stone track inclining
left. At a fork after 150m, take the gate to
the right and ascend through a wide
zigzag past gorse into a higher field. Head
through the open gateway immediately to
the left and bear west, initially by a faint
green track (with tiny Kemp Tarn to the
right) and then over a succession of small,
hummocky tops to the cairned summit of
Reston Scar (GR460987) (30 minutes).

Descend north, through a gate, to a
wide saddle. A trod continues in the same
direction through a patch of saplings
before arcing west to a kissing gate in the
wall ahead. Once through this, turn east
again before curving up a short, but steep,
bracken-covered cone – the higher of two
compact tops upon Hugill Fell

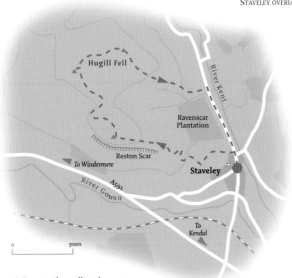

(GR459992). Drop to the wall to the east and follow it left to a kissing gate in the corner. Bear east, over a marshy depression and between small knolls, to a cairn upon the second, slightly lower (but finer, with a view along the Kentmere Valley) top (GR462993).

Strike south, close to a wall (which soon bends east) and then rake southeast down open fell to a beck by pines. Cut down the slope to a concrete driveway rising from the wooded Kentmere Road. Turn right along the road to return to Staveley (1h15).

Global reach

Reston Scar, Hugill Fell and Staveley fall just within the boundary of the Lake District National Park. If the members of the Lake District World Heritage Site Project (a partnership of public and private bodies) have their way then World Heritage Site status will soon be added to that distinction. Since 2006 the group has been preparing a bid to persuade first the government and then the United Nations Educational, Scientific and Cultural Organisation (UNESCO) of their case. There are currently 28 World Heritage Sites (defined as being of 'outstanding universal value') in the United Kingdom, including Hadrian's Wall, the Giant's Causeway, Stonehenge and the City of Bath. The bidders believe that achieving this status will significantly raise the area's international profile (admittedly already quite high) and enhance the local economy.

◀ Reston Scar rises above Staveley

Kentmere tribute

▲ **Yoke** (706m)

Distance 12km Time **4 hours 15**
Height gain **550m** Map **OS Explorer OL7**
Access parking is next to non-existent in
Kentmere, with only a handful of spaces by
the village institute adjacent to the church.
When running (the service is weekends-
only and seasonal), the 519 Kentmere
Rambler from Windermere is the answer

**Adventurers note: high above
Kentmere awaits the northeast ridge of
Rainsborrow Crag, a miniature Striding
Edge. 'A hidden gem' was how A. Harry
Griffin, the long-time Lake District
diarist of *The Guardian*, described the
ridge in 1974. The crag is almost as
unknown now as it was then, and the
stride through the valley and return by
Garburn Pass provides one of the best
ways of enjoying the Kentmere Valley.**

Start at Kentmere Church (GR456041).
Walk up the access road east of the church,
forking right after 50m onto a metalled lane
weaving between scattered cottages. Pass

through the cobbled yard at the lane end
onto a green track, leaving this (via a wall
gap) after 200m to cross a footbridge over
the River Kent. Trend left up the far bank to
a walled path and head up the valley.

As the terrain opens out, rise to a point
above the bottom house of the cluster at
Hollow Bank, picking up a metalled lane
that descends to a final farmhouse, at
Overend. A muddy lane continues
through pastures (with Rainsborrow Crag
increasingly dominant) to a barn, Tongue
House. Cut through its fold and then
break right onto a path undulating to
prominent slate heaps. Head round to the
left of these and follow a thin path
clinging to the slope above the infant
river. Some 250m short of the dam, cross a
tiny footbridge over the water and rise to
cross the elegantly stepped reservoir
outflow (1h).

Walk 50m right along the main track
and then turn west up the rough, grass
slope to the left. Initially steep, the
gradient slackens towards the skyline,

◄ Outflow beneath Kentmere Reservoir

with a beck set within a channel joined to the right. Bear SSW to the conical head of Steel Rigg, a grassy alp (with a tiny, wavy top) set within the wide combe of Rainsborrow Cove (GR442072). Contour in a southern arc around the back of the bowl to a pair of quarry ruins resting on the levelled tops of slate heaps.

A faint trod rises southeast from the lower ruin over a collapsed wall to the northern 'corner' of Rainsborrow Crag. Ascend sharply, forging a glorious line over a succession of pointed rock towers (with jutting shards of slate) and the short grassy interludes between. Do not drift around to the crag itself – keep to the corner on a SSW bearing. This is as much a steep walk as a scramble, but be watchful – the exposure is considerable (it defeats the object somewhat, but by preferring a line north of the corner the going is easier, if considerably less rewarding). The ridge culminates at a grass arête, just to the north of a deep gully. Head up the shallow trough above, slanting across the top of the gully to a shoulder decorated with a tiny tarn. It is over too soon.

Rake west up a coarse grass slope, aiming directly for the large summit cairn on Yoke (GR437067) (2h30). Leave south by a laid path along the ridge, cutting left down a steeper section to a kissing gate. Beyond, the descent – across rather dreary moorland – is gently graded, but with a good, firm path speeding the way. Arriving at Garburn Pass (identifiable by the rise to Sallows and a plantation ahead), turn left before the fence, picking up a charming drove road. Initially steep, the going eases across Crabtree Brow before the route passes through a delightful section surrounded by pines and giant boulders. Hitting the road, weave left past Greenhead and Kentmere's salubrious residences and back to the church (4h15).

Heights above Bowness

▲ **School Knott** (232m), **Brant Fell** (191m)

Distance 8km **Time 2 hours 30**
Height gain 270m **Map OS Explorer OL7**
Access the waterside at Bowness is
served by the 599 bus from Windermere
Station and Ambleside

**It is hardly any distance at all from
Bowness to School Knott and Brant Fell,
but it does not feel that way. For upon
these grassy knolls, so close to the
edge of town, the grating practicalities
of tourism – commerce, crowds and
traffic – seem a world away.**

Start in the centre of Bowness, by the
mini-roundabout at the junction of Lake
Rd and Rayrigg Rd (GR403969). Walk up
Lake Rd for 100m, then fork right onto
Helm Rd. Pass by the Windermere Hydro
Hotel and continue uphill, rounding a left-
hand bend; at a second left bend, branch
right (SP Helm Farm) along a leafy
rhododendron-lined driveway. Go straight
ahead past Helm Lodge before swinging
almost immediately right along the lane
to Helm Farm (now almost subsumed into
the town). Approaching the whitewashed
farmhouse, turn left along the edge of a
copse of young trees to a path starkly
separating orderly development from
disorderly craggy nature. After 250m bear
right, alongside a line of pristine white
bungalows, and then look right for a path
hidden at the foot of a wooded hump a
further 200m on. Follow the path to the
right of the cottages and through the field
beyond to a minor road.

Take the path opposite (SP Old
Droomer), descend through a soggy field
to a footbridge and walk up steps to a lane.
Turn left, following the lane to a high deer
gate, which opens on to the beginnings of
community woodland. Bear east (SP
School Knott) to a gate into access land,
then southeast over open springy turf to
the summit of School Knott (GR425974),
which has a great outlook over the town
and lake.

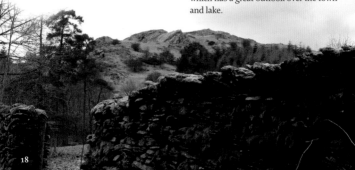

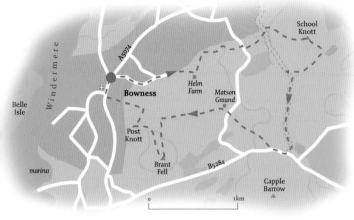

Traverse the top, descending southeast to the edge of School Knott Tarn. Head WSW over the low brow to the right and down to the corner of the field, joining a stony, gorse-fringed track (1h15). Coming to a more even surface (classified as a 'byway open to all traffic' – look out for trials bikers, etc.), turn left, continuing south on the track until it reaches a metalled lane. Wind along the length of the lane, past a scatter of residences, to reach the side of the B5284. Keep to the right of the road (a stile on the right gives access to a path largely avoiding the road itself).

Turn up the next driveway and take the left fork ('Low Cleabarrow'). Just before the house, branch left into a field (SP Dales Way) and then right down the slope to a pair of gates. Crest the lovely wooded brow beyond and roll northwest across glorious parkland to a narrow minor road. From the kissing gate opposite, follow a fenced route past Matson Ground stables and over a farm track to a path sandwiched between a pond and trees. Briefly take a metalled lane, bearing right and then, after 25m, turn off it to the left. Cut west through handsome fields and over an access road to a short walled lane at the edge of trees. Through the gate at its far end, turn left up steps to a steep grass bank, weaving to the top of a wooded knoll, where a path runs to a stile out to open ground. It is now an easy ascent SSE to the top of the grassy cone of Brant Fell (GR409961).

Return initially in the general direction of the stile, then look to the left of a small plantation for a ladder stile straddling the western wall. Go over this and walk west to a wonderful viewpoint, Post Knott, high above the lake. Turn north into woods, curving down onto a path contouring to a junction with the Dales Way. Join the long-distance walkers for a final descent to and down Brantfell Rd, into the bustle of Bowness (2h30).

Town to town

▲ **Orrest Head** (238m)

Distance 9km Time **2 hours 30**
Height gain **300m** Map **OS Explorer OL7**
Access **Windermere Station, arguably the
principal terminus of the Southern Lakes,
with connections to many destinations**

**There is much more above the head of
Windermere than the Southern Lakes'
two busiest towns, as this intricate linear
expedition along ancient lanes and
through sleepy pastures reveals.**

Start by Windermere Station (GR413986).
Walk down the A591 for 50m and cross, jink
around the railings and take the metalled
lane ahead, as directed by the pointing
finger sign for Orrest Head. Follow the lane
as it climbs a wooded hillside, first
through zigzags then raking northwest
along a terrace. At the road end, branch
right through open woodland, rising to a
path contouring inside the top edge of the
trees. Turn right along the path, through a
kissing gate and up a pitched path to the
rocky crown of Orrest Head (GR414993).

Descend north to a wall junction; go
through the stile to the right and undulate
downwards – parallel to the wall to the
left – across a hummocky field. Coming
to a narrow back road, turn right. After
200m, bear off into the field to the left
(SP Far Orrest). Keep left of the farm
buildings, clipping the edge of a tiny
copse and then head northwest,
traversing four bucolic pastures towards
Far Orrest Farm. Cross a green lane and
walk right of the farm to a walled path.
Rise back to open pasture – with
scattered pines to the left and the
knobbly mound of Allen Knott (worth
the detour) to the right – and walk north
to a green track gradually descending to
Moorhowe Road. Turn downhill and
follow the road for 750m to its junction
with the A592 (1h15).

Cross to the pavement opposite and
walk right for 75m to a kissing gate. Drop
through the field to the dual footbridges
over Trout Beck and then ascend to its
namesake village. Cross straight over the
road to the driveway by Town End, rise
through the gate at its top and incline
left by a narrow path at the rim of trees
to another road. Turn left and then bear

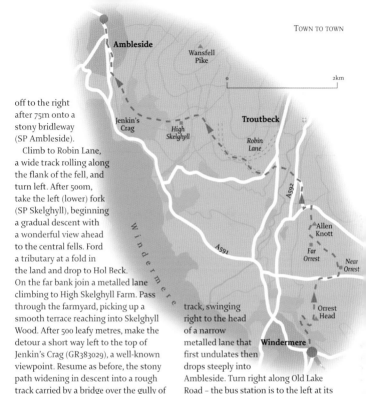

off to the right after 75m onto a stony bridleway (SP Ambleside).

Climb to Robin Lane, a wide track rolling along the flank of the fell, and turn left. After 500m, take the left (lower) fork (SP Skelghyll), beginning a gradual descent with a wonderful view ahead to the central fells. Ford a tributary at a fold in the land and drop to Hol Beck. On the far bank join a metalled lane climbing to High Skelghyll Farm. Pass through the farmyard, picking up a smooth terrace reaching into Skelghyll Wood. After 500 leafy metres, make the detour a short way left to the top of Jenkin's Crag (GR383029), a well-known viewpoint. Resume as before, the stony path widening in descent into a rough track carried by a bridge over the gully of Stencher Beck. Continue down by the track, swinging right to the head of a narrow metalled lane that first undulates then drops steeply into Ambleside. Turn right along Old Lake Road – the bus station is to the left at its end, on Kelsick Rd (2h30).

A railway town

Windermere (the town) is entirely a creation of the railway age. Before the arrival of the steam engines in 1847, it was little more than a scattered hamlet, known as Birthwaite. The name of the lake was adopted for the new town for purely commercial reasons, being a more evocative name to sell to the Victorians escaping the grime of the industrial cities for holidays and daytrips in the clean, restorative air of the Lakes. This was the democratisation of the Lakes: though guidebooks to the area had circulated since the latter half of the 18th century, these had little impact beyond those who were moneyed and/or adventurous enough to make the journey. Readily accessible by train, and at a reasonably modest cost, the town burgeoned, driven as much by tourism then as it is now.

◀ Looking west from Moorhowe Road   21

All's well on Wansfell

▲ **Wansfell Pike** (482m)

Distance 7km **Time** 2 hours 30
Height gain 440m **Map** OS Explorer OL7
Access the bus station on Kelsick Rd sees traffic from Kendal, Carlisle, Keswick and numerous other places

Scale a stone staircase to Wansfell Pike, then make a wonderful rolling traverse of the fell top before returning through the National Trust's Skelghyll Wood. Along the way, enjoy some of the best views across the waters of Windermere.

Start at the Market Cross, Ambleside (GR376045). Walk south by the A591 for 300m, branch left onto Old Lake Road and turn up Blue Hill Road after a further 200m. Climb between higgledy-piggledy cottages stacked along the hillside and through more modern housing, following the road to its head at the edge of a wood. Trend left with a path at the bottom edge of the trees to a walled lane traversing open fellside (with the summit of Wansfell Pike in view high to the right). Coming to a junction with a rising and well-worn path, turn directly up the slope and make a steepening ascent by a largely pitched path. Move through a gap in the wall to the left and continue ahead to the summit knoll (GR394041), heading left to complete the ascent (1h).

Return to the shoulder just south of the summit and go through a stile. Roll south, shadowing the wall on a narrow green path. After 250m, as the descent steepens,

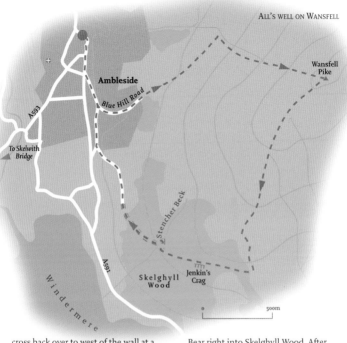

cross back over to west of the wall at a
ladder stile. Join a more distinct green
path meandering broadly SSW over softly
folded, rock-broken ground, guided
occasionally by 'permitted path' markers.
By the fenced remains of what was
probably once a tiny quarry (with anyway
an impressive cairn), the route morphs
into a grassy track leading through two
five-bar gates. Beyond the second, ignore
a marker pointing west and stick with the
track into a final field. Turn south, staying
to the left of a wall down to a terrace
carrying the bridleway between Skelghyll
and Ambleside.

Bear right into Skelghyll Wood. After
500m, be sure to detour the short way left
to the top of Jenkin's Crag (GR383029),
a rock platform peeking out of the trees
that affords a celebrated view over the
lake. Resume as before, descending
through lovely woodland by a stony path
widening into a rough track to cross the
bridge over the gully of Stencher Beck.
Continue down by the track, swinging
right to the head of a narrow metalled
lane that first undulates then drops
steeply back to Old Lake Road. Turn right
to return to the bright lights of
Ambleside (2h30).

◀ Serpentine Windermere from the southern flank of Wansfell

Falls of Ambleside

**Distance 7.5km Time 2 hours 15
Height gain 270m Map OS Explorer OL7
Access the bus station on Kelsick Rd sees
traffic from Kendal, Carlisle, Keswick and
numerous other places**

Of the things to see on the slopes above
Ambleside, woods and water top the
list. In autumn, after heavy rain (which
is not unheard of), when the water is
particularly white and the leaves
particularly golden, and when perhaps
the sun is shining (so not too much to
ask for!), this gentle exploration is the
finest walk to be had from the town.

Start at Market Cross, Ambleside
(GR376045). Walk right by the A591 for
50m to the sharp, right-hand bend, and
then take the lane opposite, reaching
behind Barclays Bank and raking left (SP
'To the Waterfalls'). Follow tree-lined

Stock Ghyll Lane, rising to a gate into
Stock Ghyll Park. Head up through the
woods to view the cascading falls of Stock
Ghyll Force. On reaching the top of the
path, fork right to rejoin the road.

Continue upwards, gaining an elevated
road bobbing across the hillside. Just past
the cattle grid by Low Grove Farm, turn
down a muddy path back to the ghyll;
cross the footbridge, follow the water
downstream for 100m and then rake back
up to Roundhill Farm. Take the farm's
access lane to Kirkstone Road, from which
there is a view back over the town and
to the lake.

Wander down Kirkstone Road for 150m
to a leafy S-bend, where a walled path
splits off to the right. This leads into an
undulating lane high above the town;
after three stiles, head down a driveway,
across the road end and along the lane

◀ Stock Ghyll Force

beyond. Coming to a steep road
(1h), turn sharply upwards,
through a five-bar gate to a
stony walled lane climbing
the hillside. As this levels
off, it dives (for 700m)
into glorious woodland
above Scandale Beck.

Just above a series of
whitewater cascades, the
path emerges from the trees to
reach High Sweden Bridge. Cross
the delicate arch and climb WSW
up the far bank, over a ladder stile
and on for 100m to a sheepfold.
Go through a gap in the wall to
the left and begin a rolling descent
south over rough pastures.

A green track slowly emerges,
evolving into a solid way twisting
down to Low Sweden Bridge. Cross back
over the beck and curve up to Nook End
Farm, joining metalled Nook Lane. Follow
the lane on a gradual descent back into
Ambleside, past the buildings (both old

and new) of the University of Cumbria.
At a T-junction, turn left past the Golden
Rule pub and then right down Smithy
Brow to return to Market Cross (2h15).

Stock Ghyll Force

As he records in a letter, a visit to Stock Ghyll Force made a powerful impression upon the young poet John Keats (1795-1821): 'The falls have as different characters; the first darting down the slate rock like an arrow; the second spreading out like a fan – the third dashed out into a mist – and the one on the other side of the rock a sort of mixture of all these. We afterwards moved away a space, and saw nearly the whole more mild, steaming silverly through the trees. What astonishes me more than anything is the tone of the colouring, the slate, the stone, the moss, the rock-weed; or, if I may say so, the intellect, the countenance of such places. The space, the magnitude of mountains and waterfalls are well imagined before one sees them; but this countenance or intellectual tone must surpass every imagination and defy any remembrance'.

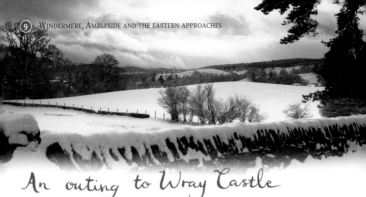

An outing to Wray Castle

Distance 10.5km **Time** 2 hours 45
Height gain 120m **Map** OS Explorer OL7
Access the 505 Coniston Rambler, linking
Ambleside and Coniston, calls in at
Hawkshead. The 'Green Cruise'
(Windermere Lake Cruises) stops by
request at Wray Castle, but does not collect

**Down shady lanes and rolling pastures
this is a slice of another, rather sedate part
of the Lakes, a bygone landscape in the
western shadow of Windermere, dotted
with farms and home to a fantasy castle.**

Start in the centre of Hawkshead, by the
Beatrix Potter Gallery (GR352981). Walk
under the archway into Red Lion Square
and down to the B5285. Follow the lane
opposite, past cottages, to the bridge over
Black Beck at its end. Skirt left around the
field and then rise northeast over
pastures. Reaching a walled path (Scar
House Lane), turn right and then left
through a stile after 150m, making a short
climb up to a knot of trees. Over a stile at
the top, head east towards a whitewashed
house, rounding right of it to join a lane
rising left through peaceful Crag Wood.

Shadow a wall to the left out of the trees
and up to a road (Loanthwaite Lane),
turning left.

Just past High Loanthwaite Farm, bear
right onto a track, then immediately left
(SP Outgate). Cross a pair of fields, the
second leading into sparse hummocky
woods. Continue north over an open
depression and up to the edge of Outgate,
passing behind houses on a grassy path
to emerge at the road by the Outgate Inn.
Turn right and follow the narrow B5286
over a bad brow and out of the village to
a sharp bend to the left. Branch right onto
a walled bridleway – the stony path
descends at the edge of woods (Spicka
Coppice) to open ground close to sleepy
Blelham Tarn. Continue northeast along
a characterful green way (running parallel
to the tarn, 200m from it), over stepping-
stones and into woods. Carry on in the
same direction through a final hillock-
scattered field to the road.

Head downhill to Low Wray Bridge and
then left on the lane to the National Trust
campsite. Just before the first (elegant)
building on the estate, bear right onto a

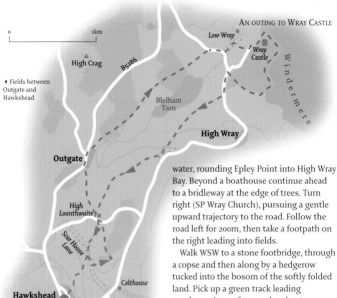

0   1km

High Crag

B5286

Low Wray

Wray Castle

Windermere

◄ Fields between Outgate and Hawkshead

Blelham Tarn

Outgate

High Wray

High Loanthwaite

Scar House Lane

Colthouse

Hawkshead

Priest Pot

wide path leading east up to the main drive of Wray Castle. Turn left towards the castle itself, a squat and rather gaunt neogothic bulk (which may be explored from the outside, though not inside). Across from the portico (GR374010), steps drop to a laid path winding down by a metal fence to the lake. Walk ahead for 100m to admire the shabby grandeur of the castle boathouse, seemingly melting into its surroundings (1h30).

Shadow the lake shore south through woods to the tiny rocky spit of Watbarrow Point, a fine place from which to view the sailboats. Continue over the wooded hill into parkland and stride back down to the

water, rounding Epley Point into High Wray Bay. Beyond a boathouse continue ahead to a bridleway at the edge of trees. Turn right (SP Wray Church), pursuing a gentle upward trajectory to the road. Follow the road left for 200m, then take a footpath on the right leading into fields.

Walk WSW to a stone footbridge, through a copse and then along by a hedgerow tucked into the bosom of the softly folded land. Pick up a green track leading southwest into a farmyard and onto a metalled lane; head uphill for 100m before swinging right onto a gravel lane (SP Outgate) to High Tock How. Split left before the farm, first to a gate and then through a kissing gate in the wall to the left a further 100m on. Cross southwest over a lovely, undulating and moundy field into the next one, then ford a stream and bear diagonally left to a track to High Loanthwaite. Walk along the road past the farm, turning off to the right just past the barn (SP Hawkshead). A narrow laid path at the field edge descends with the village in sight. At Scar House Lane, jink left and then right after 30m to resume a descent through the fields. Cross back over Black Beck and the B5286 to return to the squares of Hawkshead (2h45).

Near and Far

Distance 6km **Time** 1 hour 45
Height gain 140m **Map** OS Explorer OL7
Access during the summer months, the
best response to the chronic shortage of
parking in the Sawreys is to jump on the
seasonal public transport. As part of the
525 'Cross Lakes Experience', Mountain
Goat operates a service between
Hawkshead and Ferry House on the west
shore of Windermere, stopping in Near
Sawrey and connecting with the ferry
from Bowness

**Step aside Beatrix Potter! The real star
in the vicinity of the Sawreys is the
virtually unknown Moss Eccles Tarn
(which, admittedly, was a gift made by
Potter to the National Trust) – a study in
languid serenity.**

Start at the entrance to the small
National Trust car park in the centre of
Near Sawrey (GR369956). Walk towards
Hawkshead along the B5285, turning left

down a narrow side road just past Sawrey
House B&B. Descend out of the village,
following the road as it contours around
the hillside to a fork, and bear left
('Single Track Road'). Pass Dub How
Farm, continue along the very quiet,
hedgerow-lined road for a further 500m to
the edge of trees, and then turn left
through a pair of five-bar gates. Follow the
path through the woods, inclining right
then levelling out and weaving northeast
to a kissing gate at the far edge of the
trees. Descend gradually in the same
direction across a long pasture and
through successive gates to a lovely
terrace clinging to the northern edge of
the field beyond. Drop to the road, turn
left and walk past the scattered cottages
and church into Far Sawrey.

Where the road splits, take the left fork
up to the B5285, crossing to the narrow no
through road opposite. Crest the brow
and follow the lane up to its end at a

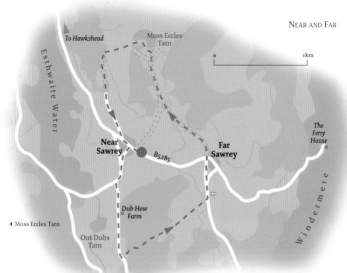

◄ Moss Eccles Tarn

cattle grid (1h), continuing along the track beyond into the field. After 100m this forks – go left, over a beck, to climb by trees to a meeting with another (walled) track. Continue ahead (north), making generally upward progress for 550m. As the wall to the left withdraws, ascend the short grass slope between it and a rock or to emerge at the southern tip of Moss Eccles Tarn (GR372967).

Follow the National Trust's permissive (and initially duckboarded) path winding along the wooded southern edge of the tarn to a kissing gate and then open country. Rise to the top of the grass slope ahead (bearing left of a rock outcrop) for a panoramic view over Esthwaite Water, before descending west through parkland, over a ruined wall and down to a track shadowing this side of the far boundary wall. Bear south along the track, soon reaching the head of a metalled single-track lane rising from Near Sawrey. A stroll down its length brings you back to the B5285 at the western tip of the village (1h45).

The conifers of Claife

Ennerdale is generally held to be the Lake District's most notorious example of inappropriate afforestation. An alternative nomination would be Claife Heights, a low, wavy upland overlooking the west shore of Windermere, ruined by a depressing maze of gloomy conifers, tightly jostling Christmas trees, dismal stumps and churned ground. Mercifully, the country just to the south around Moss Eccles and Wise Een Tarn escaped the treatment, its beauty and charm giving a bittersweet hint of how the heights must once have been.

29

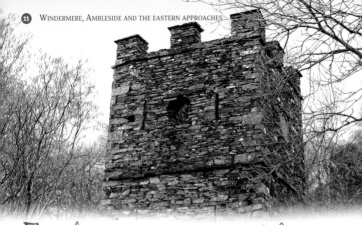

Finsthwaite figure-of-eight

**Distance 7.5km Time 2 hours 15
Height gain 290m Map OS Explorer OL7
Access both the X35 (running between
Barrow-in-Furness and Kendal) and the
618 (from Ambleside and Windermere)
stop in Newby Bridge**

In the woods above the southern tip of
Windermere, unexpected treasures await:
from a Gothic stone tower dedicated to
the derring-do of 18th-century sailors
to a pair of unheralded and rather
prosaically-named tarns, Low and High
Dam, twinkling pearls among the foliage.

Start by the Swan Hotel, Newby Bridge
(GR369864). Walk by the road in the
direction of Lakeside, over the railway
bridge and then immediately left along an
access lane. After 25m, turn up to the right
(SP Summer House Knott) along a stone
staircase between garden boundaries. Pass
through the gate at the head into native

woods, following a wallside path towards a
dip in the skyline by thinning trees. Just
below this, rake sharply right with the
path, then curve back up to the left, forking
left by a marker post along the 'public right
of way'. It is now a short climb to the top
of Summer House Knott, distinguished by
the memorial tower, a picturesque
castellated folly (GR370869) (20 minutes).

Take the permitted path just to the west
of the tower, bearing NNE through lovely
rolling woodland. Just beyond a gap in a
mossy wall, at a junction with a forestry
track running north-south, turn left
(north), meandering downwards through
pines. At a fork go left, as directed by a red
arrow, to reach a path running within the
edge of the canopy. Turn left, out of the
woodland and across two pastures,
towards handsome Finsthwaite Church
with its distinctive spire.

From the road end, pass the village hall

◄ Memorial tower,
Summer House Knott

and bear left at the fork just beyond the church. Jink right at the junction and then left after 20m onto a path by cottages leading into an open field. Bear north to a second, hummocky field – graced by a scattering of static caravans – and slant upwards towards a gate in the far corner. Enter the access area, cross the beck into woods and turn upstream beside the water. The path eventually merges into a much larger one leading up to a gate; go through this and fork left (SP Permitted Path), ascending to the lip of Low Dam, a tranquil tree-lined pool. Skirt to its right and rise up the grassy bank ahead (the dam of High Dam), which is topped by a low wall.

Walk over the dam and make a clockwise circuit of the tarn. For the first third or so this follows the shore, then, beyond Little Mire Beck, the path moves away from the water (do not be distracted by the path climbing directly away to the left though), gaining an elevated line 20m or so above the water. A hint of moorland briefly intrudes by the drop into a marshy area north of the tarn before the trees are re-entered along the eastern edge. Back by the dam (1h30), cross the bridge over the outlet (GR363886) and retrace the route through the woods and fields back to Finsthwaite.

Return to the church, where a path splits right before the road end into a succession of long green pastures. Head SSW, on a constant gentle rise, holding a steady line to a ladder stile at the final field end into the woods at Wintering Park. Bear diagonally left on a good path, through a dip and over a crest before descending steeply in the same direction. Leave the trees by a path sandwiched between private gardens to find yourself back on the access lane taken at the beginning of the walk (2h15).

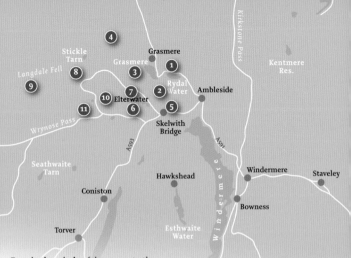

Even in the minds of those new to the Lake District, the names Grasmere and Langdale are somehow familiar, evoking a romantic image of vigorous and luxuriant nature. This is the Lakes of the imagination: still blue waters, sinuous green valleys, dark slate walls, rust-brown fellsides and charcoal-shaded mountains. Reality does not always accord with these visions – car parks tend not to feature – but there is something about the way Silver How roughly backgrounds Grasmere or the Langdale Pikes soar from the end of their namesake valley that is irresistible and, yes, romantic.

The spirit of Grasmere is emphatically poetic. Nowhere else can the shadow of a poet be so long. Wordsworth is everywhere, but the only real way to understand his connection to the environment, and the inspiration he drew from it, is to leave the town itself and head into the hills. Feel the breeze across Silver How, Nab Scar or Tarn Crag and see if something of that Wordsworth feeling persists.

Red Bank – the pass across the shoulder separating Grasmere and Great Langdale – makes for a charming walk and a hairy drive. Either way, Great Langdale is worth it. Not for the strangely characterless valley floor itself (distinguished only by the view from it), but for the magnificence of the surrounding hills and mountains. The challenges and delights are many and varied: Jack's Rake on Pavey Ark is a serious undertaking, the Climber's Traverse on Bowfell demands sure feet, while lower down Blake Rigg and Lingmoor provide mountain adventures in miniature. Indeed, climb anywhere above Langdale and a false note is almost impossible to find.

GRASMERE AND THE LANGDALES

In Romantic footsteps

Distance 6km **Time** 2 hours 30
Height gain 420m **Map** OS Explorer OL7
Access White Moss Common may
be reached by the 555 bus, which zips
along the A591 between Keswick
and Windermere

With Rydal Mount at one end and Dove
Cottage at the other, the 'coffin route'
between Grasmere and Rydal (there being
no graveyard in Rydal) is a trail rich in
Wordsworth associations. Hidden from
the nearby bustle, it is also virtually
unchanged since the great man regularly
walked this way. Combined with the
outlook above Nab Scar and with Mr
Alcock's serene tarn, it is the perfect way to
follow in the footsteps of the Romantics.

Start at the lower White Moss car park,
just south of the A591 by Rydal Water
(GR350065). Walk by the road towards
Grasmere for 75m and then cross to a track
alongside a beck. At a fork bear right and
follow a stony-bedded walled lane to the
'coffin route', which contours along the

valley edge between Grasmere and Rydal.
This is the way the deceased parishioners
of Rydal came on their final journey en
route for burial at Grasmere. Turn left and
follow it for 250m to the indent by Dunney
Beck. Turn through the gate and rise left of
the water for 200m to where the Thirlmere
Aqueduct cuts across. Leave the beck here
and traverse west along a thin path,
brushing the top of a plantation. Locate an
old metal pedestrian gate, set distinctively
in the wall rising ahead, and climb up to it
(but not through it). Briefly shadow the
wall until it bends away to the left, then
strike out north over enjoyably rough
terrain. Having turned into little more
than a sheeprun, the path bypasses a
large sheepfold to reach a wall stile with,
beyond, a much larger path drifting the
short way up to Alcock Tarn.

Cross the dam at the southern end of
the tarn and go through a gap in the wall
to the east, from where a path inclines
southeast across the fellside to a
prominent cairn on the skyline. Gaining

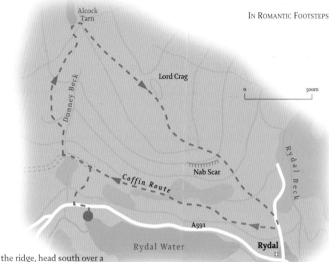

the ridge, head south over a ladder stile to top the fiercely steep slope plunging south (Nab Scar, the truncated end of the long ridge extending all the way north to Fairfield). There is a wonderful, precipitous view over Rydal to Loughrigg.

Descend southeast by a worn and failsafe path (popularised by the Fairfield Horseshoe), steepening in its middle reaches. A shelf, just above a series of wide, engineered zigzags, offers a second viewpoint to rival, if not better, that from the top. Beyond a ladder stile, follow much narrower zigzags to the edge of Rydal. Join a concrete track, which leads onto a metalled road, and then 50m on bear right on a sheltered bridleway (SP Grasmere) leaving between cottages.

Back on the 'coffin route', cut across the bottom of the fellside on a charming undulating line, balanced between old woods, velvet pastures and the rust and charcoal-tinted face of Nab Scar. 1.5km out of Rydal, just through a gate with an ornate handle, you find yourself back at the junction with the outward path rising from the A591. Turn down the path for the short walk back to the car park (2h30).

Poetry in Grasmere

Based at Dove Cottage, Grasmere, The Wordsworth Trust (wordsworth.org) does a great job sustaining the creative legacy of the Lakes' Poets. In a programme of fortnightly events running from April to October, the trust's 'Poetry in Grasmere' season draws together the country's leading poets with an eclectic mix of overseas writers and emerging talents. It is, according to former Poet Laureate Andrew Motion, 'The best poetry programme in Britain'.

Light and shade by Grasmere

Distance 5km Time 1 hour 30
Height gain 110m Map OS Explorer OL7
Access White Moss Common may be
reached by the 555 bus, which plies its
trade along the A591 between Keswick
and Windermere

Think twice about this route on a bank holiday weekend when the crowds will be suffocating, but out of season or late on a summer evening, as the sun sets and dusk falls, Loughrigg Terrace, Red Bank Wood and the shore of Grasmere make for one of the best lazy strolls in the Lakes.

Start at the lower White Moss car park, just south of the A591 by Rydal Water (GR350065). Walk along the strolling path leaving from the far (western) point of the car park, going left at the fork, to a footbridge. Cross the River Rothay and follow the path ahead (SP Loughrigg Terrace), weaving through stately woods up to a kissing gate in its southern edge. Turn right along the wallside path beyond the gate, and around an S-bend to a brow. Branch left up the straight path – Loughrigg Terrace – that inclines genteelly across the base of the fell towards Red Bank. A famed Lakes' panorama opens: to Grasmere (the lake), Helm Crag and up the valley to the pass at Dunmail Raise. Midway along the terrace is the place to pause, with the thought that perhaps everyone ever associated with the Lakes has probably stood there.

Through the metal National Trust gate at the top of the terrace, continue ahead along a shady lane through woodland. Ignore the path leaving right (SP

Grasmere) and continue ahead to a fork 100m on, taking the lower (right) option. Approaching the road, rise to it by steps to the right and then continue right along it, picking up a narrow path leaving from the opposite side 50m on (SP Grasmere). Pass through another gate and back into trees, this time the glorious Red Bank Wood. Contour around a steep and spectacular little amphitheatre, scattered with upended, moss-covered trunks, and around the next spur to an old lane raking down the hillside. Travelling down the partially pitched lane between thickly mossed walls (everything is mossy on Red Bank), you feel as though you have fallen through a rabbit hole of time, as if

Coleridge is about to appear around the next bend.

The track merges into a metalled access lane and continues down to meet the road again. Turn right along the road for 125m and then left down a laid path to the lake (1h). Shadow the placid water's edge for 800m into woods, drop to the shore and pass through a gate onto a pebble beach looking across the lake to Helm Crag. Continue past the weir at the outlet of the Rothay, crossing the river at the footbridge. Take the path slanting up to the right into Penny Rock Wood, crest the brow, descend to the riverside and join the path sweeping back to the car park, past the bridge crossed at the beginning of the walk (1h30).

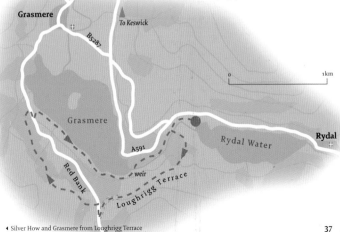

◀ Silver How and Grasmere from Loughrigg Terrace

The rough side of Silver How

▲ **Silver How** (395m)

Distance 5.5km Time **2 hours 15**
Height gain **345m** Map **OS Explorer OL7**
Access **the frequent 555 service connects
Grasmere to Keswick, Ambleside and
Windermere, and to all sorts of places to
the south, including Kendal and Lancaster**

Up on Silver How it is the journey that
matters, not the arrival. There may be an
anonymity to its grassy summit, but the
characterful and craggy eastern flank
overlooking Grasmere makes for some
fascinating and beautiful explorations,
whether ascending alongside Wray Gill,
or descending to Kelbarrow.

Start in the centre of Grasmere, at the
northern corner of the Red Lion Hotel
(GR336075). Walk northwest on the 'no
through road' to Allan Bank, between the
gracious pillars at the road end and up the
metalled driveway. Branch right at the fork

before the house and follow a track by the
edge of trees west towards a knot of
cottages. Split left just before these onto a
path (SP Silver How & Langdale) rising
into a walled lane. Coming to open fell,
ascend with the path for 100m and then
bear left to follow the intake wall on a
traverse SSE to Wray Gill.

Cross the beck and head sharply
upstream by a jumble of rocks, trying to
stay as close as possible to the ledge
above the cascades – an enjoyably rugged
ascent. The going eases and the gradient
slackens into a juniper-flecked gill and a
junction with the main path. Turn left
along this, bearing south behind an initial
line of crags into a grassy bowl. Trend left
to gain higher ground and, beyond, the
summit knoll (GR324066) (1h15).

Undulate broadly south over two small
cairned tops. Move east off the second to
descend over some rough and steep

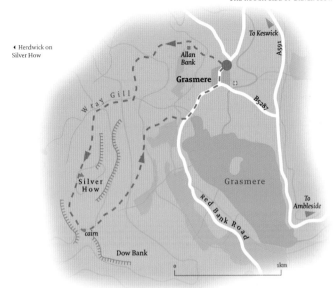

◀ Herdwick on
Silver How

ground to a large cairn at the beginning of a long low shoulder. This is the top of a pass between Langdale and Grasmere, rising by Meg's Gill above Chapel Stile and falling east of the crags of Silver How. Head north, winding down the slope past sporadic patches of gorse. Pick up a wall to the right and descend beneath the steep, scree-strewn eastern flank of Silver How. The path is clear and charming, passing through two swing gates to a narrow walled lane. Follow this to Red Bank Rd, turning left to walk the short way back into Grasmere (2h15).

Herdwicks

For a fleeting moment in 2001, as foot and mouth disease grimly advanced upon the Lakes, the unthinkable was thought: what would the fells be like without Herdwick sheep? As much a part of the furniture of the Lakes as whitewashed farmhouses, Herdwicks are remarkable and resilient animals, grazing freely around the high fells and rarely straying. Conditioned to the harsh climate of the region (and therefore cherished by the local farmers), Herdwicks can forage on the fells throughout the year without the need for supplementary feeding. The breed's distinctive grey fleece dries out more quickly than that of a white-fleeced sheep too (which is useful in the Lakes), though being coarse is suitable for use only in carpets.

39

Splendid isolation

▲ **Tarn Crag** (550m)

Distance 9.5km **Time** 3 hours 15
Height gain 500m **Map** OS Explorer OL7
Access the frequent 555 service connects,
in the first instance, Keswick, Ambleside
and Windermere to Grasmere

**Although the prospect may seem fanciful
at first glance, Easedale offers the
opportunity to do a little lonely
wandering (albeit briefly). For beyond the
well-worn trail to Sourmilk Gill and
Easedale Tarn glowers Tarn Crag, with its
tapering, wedge-shaped and barely
trodden ridge.**

Start in the centre of Grasmere, at the
northern corner of the Red Lion Hotel
(GR336075). Walk northwest on the 'no-
through road' to Allan Bank, between the
pillars at the road end, then turn right
after 25m onto a National Trust permissive
path. Follow this through fields and
alongside Easedale Road to its end by
Goody Bridge, turning left onto the road.
After 300m (at a right bend just past
Easedale Lodge), cross the footbridge over

Easedale Beck, joining a path through a
copse and into a field. Initially roughly
cobbled, the path runs alongside the beck,
past New Bridge and into a second field.
With the whitewater of Sourmilk Gill in
view ahead (and Tarn Crag looming
behind), ignore the farm track and remain
in line into a third field. Back by the beck,
head to the right of a small knoll onto a
rising, sometimes pitched path. Slant
upwards around the curving hillside, over
tributaries and beneath Brinhowe Crag
to the edge of the cascades.

Ascend alongside the gill to level ground
above the falls, bearing WSW across a
rather dreary plateau before a gradual rise
to the lip of Easedale Tarn (1h), suddenly
revealed beyond a low glacial moraine.
Though the tarn is generally considered
the draw, it is Tarn Crag, rising steeply
from the water, that dominates.

Bear right and cross the stepping stones
over the gill (which may be awkward after
heavy rain) to a ribbon of path tracking the
north shore. To make the ascent, break
from the path in line with the headland

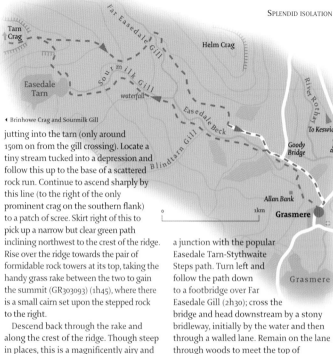

◀ Brinhowe Crag and Sourmilk Gill

jutting into the tarn (only around 150m on from the gill crossing). Locate a tiny stream tucked into a depression and follow this up to the base of a scattered rock run. Continue to ascend sharply by this line (to the right of the only prominent crag on the southern flank) to a patch of scree. Skirt right of this to pick up a narrow but clear green path inclining northwest to the crest of the ridge. Rise over the ridge towards the pair of formidable rock towers at its top, taking the handy grass rake between the two to gain the summit (GR303093) (1h45), where there is a small cairn set upon the stepped rock to the right.

Descend back through the rake and along the crest of the ridge. Though steep in places, this is a magnificently airy and wavy descent, ending at a distinctive rock crown, perched at a drunken angle. From here roll southeast down a grassy slope to

a junction with the popular Easedale Tarn-Stythwaite Steps path. Turn left and follow the path down to a footbridge over Far Easedale Gill (2h30); cross the bridge and head downstream by a stony bridleway, initially by the water and then through a walled lane. Remain on the lane through woods to meet the top of Easedale Road, either returning along its length to Grasmere or using the outward route beyond Goody Bridge (3h15).

Refreshment beckons

The best known of the Lake District's 'refreshment huts' opened by Easedale Tarn around 1870. A destination for those making the fashionable excursion from Grasmere, the small stone building was located south of the outflow, at the large boulder just left of the path. In his Tourists' Guide to the English Lakes (1880), Jenkinson wrote: 'Many persons will be annoyed on finding a small hut erected in this mountain nook, which retreat seems dedicated to solitary, pleasing reverie. Refreshments are provided by the person in charge of the hut, and a boat can be hired for a row, or a little trout fishing on the tarn'. The business survived to the Second World War, the hut then becoming a ruin before being dismantled in the 1960s.

A Loughrigg meander

▲ **Loughrigg** (335m)

Distance 6.5km **Time** 2 hours 15
Height gain 330m **Map** OS Explorer OL7
Access the 516 'Langdale Rambler' from
Ambleside makes its first stop in
Skelwith Bridge

Loughrigg is perhaps the most
fascinating low fell in the Lakes – an
otherworldly jumble of knolls, crags,
hollows and pools, criss-crossed by a
disorientating maze of tiny paths.
With its proximity to Ambleside and
Rydal, it also makes for one of the most
popular short climbs in the Lakes. Dodge
the crowds on this rugged ascent rising
from the alluring country above
Skelwith Bridge.

Start at the junction of the A593 and the
B5343 in Skelwith Bridge (GR344034). Walk
for 100m along the B5343, turn right onto
a signed footpath and rise through a field
to a walled path at the edge of woods.
Follow this to its end by Neaum Crag
holiday chalets, weaving with the access
road to the top of the development, where
a path leaves from the far end of a parking
area. From the crest, wind down a rust-
coloured slope – with a good first view of
Loughrigg and its tarn – past the bundle
of whitewashed cottages at Crag Head to
a minor road.

Turn left along the road, passing above
the tarn, to a fork after 300m. Again, keep
left, head down beside a wood and go
over the stile to the right at its end.
Undulate north through a trio of rolling
fields towards a knot of houses tucked
beneath the fellside. At the road in front
of the cottages, swing left for 25m and

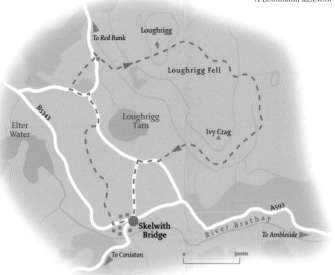

then cut back on a path inclining behind them and into trees. Walk on the level through the wood, crossing the stile at its end to find a partially pitched path climbing sharply to a cairned col. A few paces up the knoll to the left gains the summit trig point (GR347051) (1h15).

The complex geography of the fell top is now revealed. Back at the col bear ENE down a stone staircase and on to the left of a tiny tarn. Continue in the same direction down a short, steepening slope to the edge of a shallow basin, then turn southeast on an intermittent path to a depression with a lone tree. Go left from the tree, contouring ESE on a more defined path to a junction after 200m.

Turn south, quickly cutting left past a knoll, but before the top of a beck (the ominously named Black Mire). Follow the path south, skirting east around the marshy hinterland of the mire. Arriving at a much larger path, bear right to cross the beck at stepping stones.

Turn downhill (ignore the path branching left), picking up the intake wall to the left. Shadow this, bending WNW on a contour beneath Ivy Crag to a gate. Negotiate a wooded patch of tilted rock and exposed roots, joining a lane running (via a left fork) to the minor road you were on earlier. Turn right on this and then left after 250m down the narrow, steep road back into Skelwith Bridge (2h15).

◀ The alluring country above Skelwith Bridge

Bridges over the Brathay

Distance 9km **Time** 2 hours 30
Height gain 160m **Map** OS Explorer OL7
Access the 516 from Ambleside stops by
the village green in Elterwater

Contrast the two Langdales, and two
delightful ways of crossing the River Brathay,
on this dale-hopping, low-level tour through
drove lanes, handsome woods and pea-
green pastures, graced by whitewater flashes
at two memorable waterfalls – Colwith Force
and Skelwith Force.

Start at the village green in Elterwater
(GR327048). Walk south from the village,
across the roadbridge over Great Langdale
Beck and turn left at the fork. Opposite the
Elterwater Hotel, branch right up a side road,
past the lush foliage of Elterwater Hall, to
the fraying ends of the asphalt surface and
the rise of a rough stone lane. Ascend
between woods to an open shoulder
beneath the eastern fringe of Lingmoor.

The way soon descends off the ridge
into Little Langdale, passes through a gate

by cottages and morphs back into a
metalled lane. At the bottom, cross the
valley road and head down the farm lane
20m to the left, turning right into a field
(SP Slater's Bridge) just before the farm
itself. Alongside a wall to the left, drop
down with the pastures to the Brathay,
reaching the famed landmark Slaters
Bridge (GR312030) – a thin arch stooped
over the river, its rough top polished by
centuries of boots.

Walk ahead to a track running parallel to
the river behind a wall and turn left. After
400m, by a footbridge, branch right
through woods, taking the lane forking
left at the crest (SP Skelwith). The lane
becomes metalled, crosses a bridge and
rises to pass two clusters of farm
buildings, first at Stang End and then at
High Park. Just past High Park, take the
access lane and turn right before the farm
onto a path bearing east towards woods.
Entering the trees, cut down to the left on

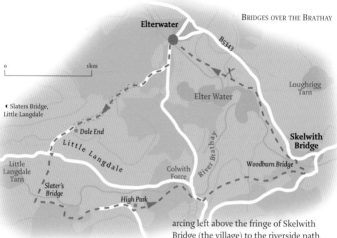

a permissive path to Colwith Force, a series of powerful whitewater cascades. Continue downstream to a junction with a minor road.

Turn right along the road and then left after 100m onto a path leading to a wooded staircase near the water. From the brow, cross rolling pastures – passing Low Park Farm – to Elterwater Park Farm. Walk through the farmyard and on to the track beyond. After 75m, split right onto a path undulating east through parkland, past a row of cottages and into woods. Descend,

arcing left above the fringe of Skelwith Bridge (the village) to the riverside path. Head upstream along the wooded bank, crossing the Brathay close to Skelwith Force at Woodburn Bridge (opened in 2007), an elegant curved steel span, topped by oak handrails.

The return to Elterwater is straight-forward, if busy in season. A laid path blazes out of the woods, over the valley pastures and alongside the otherwise tranquil bank of Elter Water (say hello to the swans). Remain next to Great Langdale Beck for a failsafe return to Elterwater (2h30).

Three Shires

When, in 1997, a wayward motorist smashed the roadside Three Shire Stone at the top of Wrynose Pass, it was a symbolic moment (if 23 years late), for the historic arrangement of counties it represented had suffered a similar fate, albeit by government decree. As the name suggests, the stone marked the meeting point of Cumberland, Westmorland and Lancashire, the three counties among which the Lakes were traditionally divided. The Brathay rises close to the stone and for its length it marked the boundary between Lancashire (to the south) and Westmorland (to the north). Happily, within a year of the accident, the Three Shire Stone was restored and returned, though unhappily for pressure groups such as the 'Friends of Real Lancashire', Cumbria persists.

Meg's Gill

Distance 7km Time 2 hours 15
Height gain 260m Map OS Explorer OL7
Access the 516 bus from Ambleside calls
at the village green in Elterwater

Blame the weather, time or inclination,
but sometimes the stellar attractions of
Great Langdale are out of reach. Do not
despair, for a wander along the valley
floor from Elterwater opens up a return
along the low, loping and wonderfully
characterful shoulder running from Meg's
Gill (a miniature gorge) to Huntingstile
Crag. Who says height matters?

Start at the village green in Elterwater
(GR327048). Walk south, across the
roadbridge over Great Langdale Beck, and
turn right along the quarry road. After
350m, opposite the fenced entrance to a
cave, branch right on a path descending to
the side of Great Langdale Beck. A short
way on, cross a footbridge back over the
beck and follow the path to the road. Turn

left, pass Wainwright's Inn and join a
stone track a further 50m on (SP
Baysbrown Campsite). Curve around to a
side road, following this left past Thrang
Farm and on to a walled path leaving right
of some cottages. With the path joining
another track after 100m, turn left again,
passing beneath an impressively large
wall (shoring up the road above) to a
rustic stone bridge (built 1818). Cross back
over the beck, and continue up the valley
along a stony track skirting the edge of a
campsite. A pleasant, if uneventful
kilometre is enlivened by a fine view of
the Langdale Pikes.

As the track veers left towards a
whitewashed cottage, make a final
crossing of the beck and walk ahead to the
valley road. Bear right, hugging the
roadside to just beyond the farm in sight
on the corner (Harry Place). Turn uphill
where the open slope rises from the road
(there is a right-of-way, but no obvious
path), drifting right to the field edge.
Soon enough, a rake is met (1h): bear right

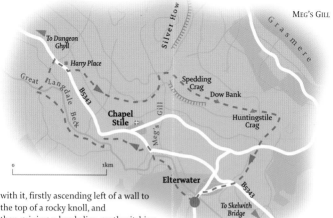

with it, firstly ascending left of a wall to the top of a rocky knoll, and then gaining a lovely line gently pitching and falling through bracken. With the rounding of a 'corner' a magnificent (and unexpected) miniature mountain scene opens, a whirl of crags and scree radiating from the falls of Meg's Gill. A thin path winds up to the left of the gill, then slants across the stream and the back of the gully before cresting at a low ridge decorated with a very prominent cairn.

Bear right (ESE) along the ridge, clinging to the southern edge of the ridge for its airy outlook over Langdale. Traverse a succession of grassy subsidiary tops: off the first, Spedding Crag, cross a small (and wet) depression, then rise over a further knoll before descending to a larger saddle (with a junction of paths). Continue ahead, over the cairned top of Dow Crag and over another marshy area to a final rise. Pass right of a drab tarn tucked beside a cracked rock tor, then descend, trending right, to a shoulder. Head down to the right, cut across the Red Bank road and choose one of the paths crossing Walthwaite Bottom to the valley road. Cross to the road back into Elterwater, where the Britannia Inn awaits (2h15).

G M Trevelyan

From leaving the road by Harry Place to regaining it at Walthwaite Bottom, the journey over the shoulder follows land belonging to the National Trust, thanks to the influential historian and academic George Macaulay Trevelyan (1876-1962). Trevelyan adored the country around Great Langdale and was fortunate enough to be able to buy up large chunks of it. Happily, he was also a committed disciple of preservation. Famed climbers' haunt The Old Dungeon Ghyll Hotel, Dungeon Ghyll itself and 700 acres of land – including the farm at Harry Place – were donated to the Trust by Trevelyan, who is more often remembered for his academic distinction (Regius Professor of Modern History at the University of Cambridge, Master of Trinity College, Cambridge, and later Chancellor of Durham University).

Langdale rocks

▲ **Pavey Ark** (698m), **Harrison Stickle** (736m), **Pike of Stickle** (709m)

Distance 7km **Time** 3 hours 45
Height gain 740m **Map** OS Explorer OL7
Access the excellent 516 bus service from Ambleside trundles up Great Langdale to the Old Dungeon Ghyll

An adrenaline-soaked scramble to rank alongside Striding Edge and Sharp Edge, Jack's Rake is one of the great mountain experiences of the Lakes. There is no better route to the knobbly trio of the Langdale Pikes either, just do not underestimate the challenge, for here is the whiff of danger.

NB: *Jack's Rake is a graded scramble (albeit Grade 1) to be approached with care. While the rock is generally good and the handholds numerous, remember the old scramblers rule of 'three points of contact'; keep a clear head and watch out for climbers, whether below or above. Steer clear in winter conditions – it's a long way down.*

Start at the large National Trust car park west of the New Dungeon Ghyll Hotel,

Great Langdale (GR294063). Walk to the top of the car park (left of the Stickle Barn pub), taking the busy tourist path rising west of Stickle Ghyll. Ascend steeply, switching banks to a largely pitched section before swapping back again at a bouldery area just beneath Stickle Tarn.

Once the tarn is reached, the cut of Jack's Rake across the glowering face of Pavey Ark is obvious, rising diagonally from bottom right (by the base of Easy Gully) to the skyline top left. Leave the crowds by the dam and follow the western shore of the tarn round to beneath the cliff, slanting upward across a line worn through scree (past a memorial inscribed 'JWS 1900') to the foot of Easy Gully (1h).

At weekends, or if you have the misfortune to arrive shortly after a large group, you may have to wait to access the rake – progress is single-file. Although the scramble cuts across the cliff face at 45 degrees, there is little sense of exposure in the lower reaches, the rake being both

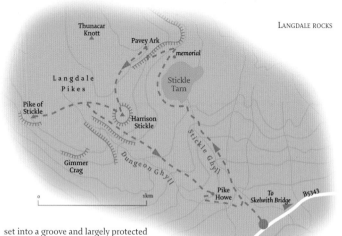

set into a groove and largely protected by a rock parapet. Some entertaining chimney moves ensue, and with the adrenaline rushing this initial section, though the steepest, is also the most stimulating. Traverse a thin grassy shelf (by Gwynne's Chimney), making an awkward move over a large fractured block at its end to reach easier, walkable ground and another, deeper groove beyond. Emerging upon an exposed platform, turn up Great Gully before trending left over rough boulders and slabs, forging a line to a dip right of a distinctive pinnacle on the skyline. The best option is then to complete the scramble over the rock to the right and up to the summit wall (GR284079).

Leave WSW from the summit, drop a few metres and contour over a blend of rough rock slabs and tufty grass in an arc curving south toward a large rock crown, the head of Harrison Stickle, an enormous buttress extending far down to the south and east. Ascend over cracked rock directly up to the

summit cairn (GR281074) (2h), the highest point of the Langdale Pikes.

Descend west by a pitched path into a shallow basin, Harrison Combe. Cross the marshy top of Dungeon Ghyll, picking up a good path undulating west to the Pike of Stickle, the most compact and handsome of the three tops. Access the summit cone from the north, scrambling up by a worn line over tilted rock to the top (GR274073) (2h30).

Retrace the route to Harrison Combe and back over the beck. Bear ESE for a sharp descent along the east rim of Dungeon Ghyll, an appropriately deep and dark ravine. An unmistakable path sweeps ESE down the initially steep and then easing slope to a subsidiary knoll, Pike How, a terrific viewpoint over Great Langdale. Descend steep ground to the intake wall, where the path draws you the short way back to the car park, or the Stickle Barn, if you prefer (3h45).

◀ The Langdale Pikes, beyond Blea Tarn and Side Pike

Bowfell's best

▲ **Bowfell** (902m)

**Distance 10km Time 4 hours 15
Height gain 810m Map OS Explorer OL6
Access the 516 bus service from
Ambleside makes it to the roadbridge by
the Old Dungeon Ghyll Hotel**

**Unfrequented routes on much-
frequented mountains are a
connoisseur's delight. For a thrilling, but
never particularly challenging take on
mighty Bowfell, say hello to the
Climber's Traverse.**

Start at the bus stop on the B5343 at the
junction with the roadbridge to the Old
Dungeon Ghyll Hotel, Great Langdale
(GR285059). Walk west to where the road
bends sharply left, continuing ahead by
the metalled access lane to Stool End
Farm. Head left through the farmyard to a
five-bar gate opening to a track. Part
company with the track 50m on and head
up the rounded foot of the ridge. A solid,

largely pitched path, broken by occasional
outcrops and patches of exposed rock,
sustains a steady ascent with bursts of
interest. Settling upon an easing line
along the southern (Oxendale) side of the
ridge – and with an impressive view of
Crinkle Crags – the path bypasses
subsidiary top White Stones to emerge
upon a grassy plateau.

Soon, as the main path begins its curve
up to the depression at Three Tarns, split
off to the right (by a cluster of four cairns)
onto a peaty trod. Continue straight up
the slope along a thin, increasingly rock-
fractured path. Reaching steeper, craggier
ground, the path turns northwest to crest
the nose of the ridge. Here the Climber's
Traverse is revealed, an undulating ribbon
strung across the steep western face,
bound for an outrageous rock cauldron.
Set off along the traverse (towards the
prominent, indented rock face – Bowfell
Buttress), hugging the base of Flat Crags

50

Angle Tarn

Stickle Tarn

Bow Fell

Climber's Traverse

Mickleden Beck

Old Dungeon Ghyll Hotel

B5343

◀ Along the Climber's Traverse

Three Tarns

Buscoe Sike

The Band

Stool End

To Skelwith Bridge

Hell Gill

Oxendale Beck

0   1km

before reaching a small combe. Trend left to rise the short way to the foot of Cambridge Crags – the cliff to the back of the combe – then turn back to the south to climb a rough stone run between it and the remarkable tilted rock shelf of Great Slab. After emerging upon gently sloping but rough and bouldery ground, cross west in the direction of the now visible top, meeting along the way the path rising from Three Tarns, an expressway to the summit dome (GR244064) (2h15). Back upon the main path, descend southeast over scattered stone to the rather forlorn Three Tarns.

Descend east from the tarns on the path back towards 'The Band'. After 50m, just past a knoll to the right, branch right over Buscoe Sike. Weave down an initial steep section to much gentler, and intermittently peaty ground, where a stride over coarse grass – with ahead an excellent view to the conical Pike of Blisco – leads to the top of Hell Gill, a narrow

and deeply incised gorge. Descend steeply in line with the southern lip of the fearsome gill, negotiating a shoddily pitched path and a badly eroded section on the way to a confluence of streams. Using the scattered rocks and boulders, ford at first left across the bottom of Hell Gill and then right over Oxendale Beck (the water level is usually not too high). An enjoyably rugged and scrambly traverse above the southern bank of Oxendale Beck follows before giving way to a green slope leading down to the main valley footbridge. Cross and follow the path downsteam, moving down to right of a wall after 400m to shadow the wide, white bed of the beck. A track is joined (sandwiched between the beck and the wall), that leads up to a sheepfold, from where it curves away back to Stool End. Return through the farmyard and along the access lane to the public road – and the temptations of the Old Dungeon Ghyll (4h15).

The great wall of Lingmoor

▲ **Brown How** (469m), **Side Pike** (362m)

Distance 6.5km **Time** 2 hours 45
Height gain 470m **Map** OS Explorer OL6
Access the 516 from Ambleside terminates
on the B5343 at the turning to the Old
Dungeon Ghyll Hotel

**Rising and falling in harmony with
typically convulsed Lake District contours,
a sturdy wall – apparently as robust as the
fell itself – marches determinedly across
the rugged top of Lingmoor. Join it, as
guide and companion, for a great mid-level
expedition to the formidable Side Pike,
with a wonderful outlook to the head of
Great Langdale.**

Start at the bus stop on the B5343 at the
junction with the roadbridge to the Old
Dungeon Ghyll Hotel, Great Langdale
(GR285059). Walk west on the road, around
the sharp left bend towards Wall End and
over the bridge 150m on. Go through a gate
immediately on the left into the National
Trust campsite, then branch right after 50m
onto a path rising through two copses.

A laid path zigzags somewhat
dispiritingly up the fellside to a ladder stile
out to the road; cross by the cattle grid to
the gate opposite, joining another laid path
for an easy stride into the conifers west of
Blea Tarn. Curve down with the path to
above the edge of the water and then, just
past the tarn, cross the footbridge left over
Bleamoss Beck. Head east along a wide
path (with a celebrated view across the tarn
to the Langdale Pikes) to meet up with the
road once again.

Bear right, over a cattle grid, turning up
the steep grass slope to the left on a
distinct trod just past a beck. Aim for a
rocky tongue set between a pair of rock
'cones' at the top of Birk Knott. With
height, drift towards the wall to the left,
shadowing it around a 90 degree bend to
the northeast. Keep next to this infallible
guide, skirting a rocky top, crossing a
depression and climbing the short way up

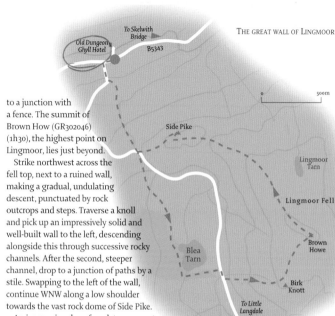

to a junction with a fence. The summit of Brown How (GR302046) (1h30), the highest point on Lingmoor, lies just beyond.

Strike northwest across the fell top, next to a ruined wall, making a gradual, undulating descent, punctuated by rock outcrops and steps. Traverse a knoll and pick up an impressively solid and well-built wall to the left, descending alongside this through successive rocky channels. After the second, steeper channel, drop to a junction of paths by a stile. Swapping to the left of the wall, continue WNW along a low shoulder towards the vast rock dome of Side Pike.

An impressive sheer face deters access to Side Pike from the east, so skirt just to its south on a thin path, passing through a narrow aperture between the pike itself and a rock finger – the so-called 'Fat Man's Agony'. A number of runs rising from the southwest and west converge into a straightforward path rising to the airy summit (GR293053) – your own Langdale eyrie. Drop down to the west, past the

point at which the climb up Side Pike began and down to the ladder stile crossed at the outset of the walk. From here, follow the laid zigzags back down into the valley, where the profile of Side Pike suggests (rather satisfyingly) it to be a more formidable conquest than it actually has been (2h45).

A Lakes Poet

When W H Auden wrote that a poet's hope was to be 'like some valley cheese, local, but prized elsewhere' he might almost have had in mind Norman Nicholson (1914-87). Earthy and direct, Nicholson's poetry drew upon the vernacular of his native Lake District and was much concerned with the tension between natural beauty and industrial waste. Observation of the area around him is a constant theme, his eye alert to the power, and rich detail, of the landscape. See his poem 'Wall' (1974) for an apposite example of his work.

◄ The wall snaking across Lingmoor   53

Freedom of the hills

▲ **Blake Rigg** (530m)

**Distance 5km Time 2 hours 15
Height gain 375m Map OS Explorer OL6
Access the 516 from Ambleside stops on
the B5343 at the turning to the Old
Dungeon Ghyll Hotel. See the preceding
walk for a route to the top of the road out
of Great Langdale**

**Discover the hill-walking maverick within
and liberation from the tyranny of paths.
Above Blea Tarn, explore the little-known
and rarely-visited Blake Rigg, an outlier of
the Pike of Blisco, taking in a wild climb
and a glorious, rolling descent. Route-
finding skills essential.**

*NB: From late spring to autumn, adventurers
ascending the gully described below will encounter
thick bracken in the lower reaches; some may prefer
to wait until the winter months.*

Start at Blea Tarn car park, off the minor
road between Dungeon Ghyll and Little
Langdale Tarn (GR295043). Cross the road
and walk down the wide path past the
southern shore of Blea Tarn. Once over the
footbridge spanning the outlet, turn left
along a path out of the trees, in line with
Bleamoss Beck. Initially shadow the
crashing waters and then contour south
away from them along a line resembling
less a path than a rough scar across a blend
of peat and rock. Join a wall to the left, crest
the brow of a small knoll and then look for
the next gully bisecting the steep slope to
the right.

Sandwiched between crags at the skyline,
the gully has a trio of holly trees in its
lower reaches, and a ruin – to the east, just
above dreary Blea Moss – marking the
point of departure from the main path.

Ascend steeply alongside the stream up the (pathless) gully, forging a way by sheepruns where practicable. Above the third holly tree, any bracken should thin a little, with a run of scree emerging above the line of the now disappeared beck. An easy scramble through the cleft between the crags noted earlier leads out from the gully to a grassy shoulder. Bear northwest, gradually gaining height over a series of small, rock-studded knolls, towards a low, conical peak, Blake Rigg, cut-off to the east by charcoal-grey crags. The top, decorated by a cairn upon angled sheets of bare rock (GR285038) (1h15), reveals a view west across the desolate plateau of Wrynose Fell to the Pike of Blisco, and to numerous tiny tarns.

Descend NNE, picking a route along grassy channels between small crags, in the direction of the distinctive truncated cone of Side Pike. A wall to the right is joined near a loose copse of windblown larches, guiding the descent. If all now appears straightforward, watch out for some large tilted sheets of exposed rock running across from the wall and – more particularly – the sheer crags, hidden from view, just below. Avoid these by moving left of the rock sheets into a shallow grass gully leading steeply down to a saddle.

Rise over a mound and continue to descend in line with the wall towards the road climbing from Great Langdale. Just before it, go through the gate to the right onto a wide laid path. An easy stride for 800m leads into the conifers west of Blea Tarn. Curve down with the path towards the water and put your feet up on one of the benches looking out over the tarn. Hop back over the outlet to return to the car park (2h15).

◄ Blake Rigg

55

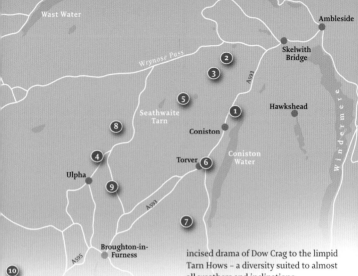

incised drama of Dow Crag to the limpid Tarn Hows – a diversity suited to almost all weathers and inclinations.

The pace drops, the population thins, and beyond Torver, hints of the teacup tourist side of the Lakes fade as the land makes its low slide out to the Irish Sea. There should be an attraction to the foot of Coniston Water, and to the low, moor-ish uplands strung between the thin valleys of the Lickle and the Duddon, simply for that reason alone. The Duddon Valley was a great favourite of Wordsworth and is still blissfully unspoilt today – the crashing of the water in Wallowbarrow Gorge is the only disturbance here.

Black Combe stands as a coda to the fells, the last bastion before the waves. The circuit around it may not be the most exciting within the Lakes but it could justifiably be claimed that the views from it are the best in the country.

Follow the main road southwest from Skelwith Bridge, crest the brow and begin the descent into Yewdale: at first glance, the southwestern Lake District begins just as the central hub ends – with striking beauty. If anything, Yewdale and the area around Tilberthwaite trump Langdale (with only the traffic along the A590 spoiling the fun), the landscape twisting and shifting with every turn through a maze of crag, wood and pasture. True, the mountains may be more hidden, and less striking from afar, but that only goes to underline the general character of the area; one that reveals itself gradually and slowly – the sort, in fact, best explored on foot.

Coniston is the grittiest of all the towns of the Lakes, with something of its no-nonsense quarryman's air still lingering. The country around ranges from the

Low Tilberthwaite ▸

CONISTON, THE DUDDON VALLEY AND OUT TO THE COAST

Man and nature

▲ Holme Fell (317m)

Distance **7.5km** Time **2 hours 30**
Height gain **280m** Map **OS Explorer OL7**
Access **Coniston, 3km distant, is as close
as Stagecoach gets, with the X12 from the
south and 505 from Ambleside**

**Take the gaping craters of a disused slate
quarry, add the most famous farmhouse
in the district, and then sandwich in
between a knobbly topped fell with a
stunning view along the length of
Coniston Water. It all makes for one
of the most compelling short walks in
the Lakes.**

Start at Tom Gill car park (GR321998),
off the A593 between Skelwith Bridge
and Coniston. Walk southwest by the
'permissive path avoiding road' to a
kissing gate opposite the entrance to Yew
Tree Farm. Cross the road and take the
wide path branching right into woods
before the farmhouse. Incline left through

the trees until they and the wall to the
right withdraw. Turn off to the right and
walk above the woods to a five-bar gate.

A distinct path leads north, undulating
between hillocks and around patches of
bog, to a fork by a large boulder; go left,
on a steepening line slanting up the
hillside. Becoming fainter the path moves
into a shallow gully – follow this directly
up to a saddle (Uskdale Gap) between
knolls on the skyline. Bear south toward a
cairned top, but do not bother to climb
this, skirting instead to its right following
a wide channel, and making for the larger
knoll to the west. Locate a narrow path
rising into a rocky groove, a breach in the
otherwise heathery and craggy slope,
leading directly to the summit of Holme
Fell (GR315006) (45 minutes).

Leave to the north and descend sharply
into a marshy basin just west of Uskdale
Gap. Forge the most practical line (a
network of sheepruns winds around the

worst of the wet) to the cluster of tiny reservoirs to the northwest. Pick-up a path around the western side of the largest (eastern) reservoir, cutting northwest through the wooded remains of a small quarry and down the good slate path beyond. Coming to a junction with a wide bridleway, turn down to the right and through a five-bar gate. Remain on the bridleway (ignore the path to Hodge Close after 300m) to its end at the Hodge Close-Oxen Fell track. Turn left and down to another gate; just after this a rocky path drops left off the lip (GR318018) into the crater of Parrock Quarry. Descend into it and walk up to the vaulted arch through which the flooded bottom of Hodge Close Quarry can be seen. This is a popular location for climbing, and the rock around the walls of the quarry may be unstable, so be vigilant.

Return by the inward route back out of the quarry and turn left, through a slate-lined cutting, to the road. Pass by cottages and then shadow, to the left of the road, the precipitous edge of the quarries (Hodge Close, in particular, is worth a tentative glance, but keep any dogs or children firmly back from the edge). Just past the craters, branch southeast back into the woods, thus completing the circuit of the quarry tops. Rejoin the bridleway used earlier and head back to the south along a glorious route – largely at the edge of the woods, but always with the perimeter wall to the right – to its end at the public road (2h). Continue downhill into the valley (with Yewdale Beck just to the right) and wander along the road, beneath the fierce, southern face of the fell, to a roadbridge over the beck. Do not cross it, but instead pick up the laid path to the left (SP Yew Tree Farm), which leads directly back to the farm. Avoid the road (other than to cross it) and walk back through the field to Tom Gill (2h30).

The four tops of Tilberthwaite

▲ **Blake Rigg** (423m), **Haystacks** (421m), **High Fell** (428m), **Great Intake** on **Low Fell** (405m)

Distance **7km** Time **2 hours 45**
Height gain **440m** Map **OS Explorer OL6 (full walk), OL7 (almost all of it)**
Access **Coniston, 4.5km distant, is as close as Stagecoach gets, with the X12 from the south and 505 from Ambleside**

In the undisturbed country north of Tilberthwaite Gill, lies a curious cluster of tiny conical fells. Hop from one to the other on this mini-exploration, opening by a dark ravine and closing near a surprising sheepfold.

Start at the National Trust car park, Low Tilberthwaite (GR306009). Walk up the steep, partially pitched path rising above the south side of Tilberthwaite Gill, ascending past impressive and rather gothic quarry workings. At a fork, bear right to a footbridge spanning the cascading gill, then rise sharply by a stone staircase up the north bank. Gain an old mine track up on a high terrace and turn left, contouring in an arc to the north. Fork right by a cairn and rise to the top of a small crest; split from the path here and climb east up the grassy bank to the right. Ascend to a shoulder and swing left, working northeast through a labyrinth of grass shelves, larch and low crags, finally following the ridge north to the unmarked summit of Blake Rigg (GR301011).

Descend north to a saddle and ascend Haystacks, a small but steep grass dome, flecked with rock and crowned by a large cairn. Drop off the top and skirt the western edge of the green bowl to the north, aiming for the small larch copse at the base of the next knoll, High Fell. Trend right, between thinning trees, to its top (GR300017).

Roam northeast, keeping above a wire fence, to the wall. Move left along the wall, shadowing it for the short stretch to a ladder stile – cross and wind upwards through bracken, drifting towards the wall to the right. Reaching the shoulder of Low Fell, swing left (northwest) and scramble up the heathery and craggy

◀ Detail of Andy
Goldsworthy's Tilberthwaite
Touchstone Fold

Greenburn Beck

Low Fell

Great Intake

Tilberthwaiten Fells

High Fell

High
Tilberthwaite

Haystacks

Blake Rigg

sheepfold

Yewdale Beck

Tilberthwaite
Gill

0   500m

summit cone of Great Intake, the finest of the four tops (GR302021) (1h30).

Between crags, pick a way off the knoll and bear west towards the last wall crossed. As the slope to the north opens, forge a line directly down to the northwest (with the help of sheepruns), picking up Birk Fell Gill and coming eventually to the stony quarry track traversing the base of the fell above Greenburn Beck. Turn right and walk ENE. After 900m, the track merges with another rising from the left; slant right, then 100m further on go right again at the fork. Ascend steadily to a crest and then undulate south, following the rough track through a charming patchwork of crags and trees for 1.5km to High Tilberthwaite Farm. Join the road just beyond the farm and turn through the first gate to the left into a pasture. Walk right of a wall, continuing in the same direction through a second field to a gate to a wooded knoll. Through this, turn immediately right along a thin path weaving through the trees, soon descending with it to reach the side of Yewdale Beck. Head upstream to return to the car park (2h45).

A sheepfold with a difference

Across from the car park, in the roadside field just south of Yewdale Beck, there is a sheepfold. So what, you say. The Tilberthwaite Touchstone Fold, however, is one of 13 folds (or groupings of folds) in Cumbria rebuilt by the sculptor Andy Goldsworthy. Making a vivid restatement of the connection between man and the land, and of the area's farming traditions, Goldsworthy added a distinct feature to each fold, in the case of the one at Tilberthwaite, four slate sculptures set in its walls.

On the edges of Wetherlam

▲ **Wetherlam** (762m)

Distance 7km **Time** 3 hours 15
Height gain 630m **Map** OS Explorer OL6
Access Coniston, 4.5km distant, is as close
as Stagecoach gets, with the X12 from the
south and 505 from Ambleside

**Taste the wild side of pock-marked
Wetherlam, arriving and departing by its
steep eastern edges for the best mountain
adventure between Langdale and
Coniston.**

Start at the National Trust car park, Low
Tilberthwaite (GR306009). Walk up the
steep, partially pitched path rising
southwest along the south side of
Tilberthwaite Gill. Ascend steadily, past
impressive and picturesque quarry
workings, to a small rock cleft with level
ground beyond, high above the precipitous
depths of the gill.

Curve around to the northwest (in line
with the gill), contouring along a narrow

path across peaty ground. Just before a
footbridge (and adjacent to an old mine
shaft), leave the path and climb west, over a
rough grassy bank strewn with rock
outcrops, to the tip of a rounded ridge,
Steel Edge (a name that in the lower
reaches hardly rings true). Gaining
definition with height, the ridge tapers and
narrows, with a trod emerging that runs
southwest along the crest up to the foot of
a sharp slope. A lengthy, entertaining and
possibly 'steely' scramble unfolds, with the
knobbly rock right of the main scree
channel generally preferable.

With a sudden shift, the climb terminates
on a rather dreary moorland plateau – bear
west, picking up the main path by a small
tarn next to a tor (1h15). Turn NNW up the
gently graded and broad south ridge,
reaching the cairned rock dome at the
summit (GR288011) after a pleasant if
uneventful kilometre.

Make a sharp, scrambly descent between

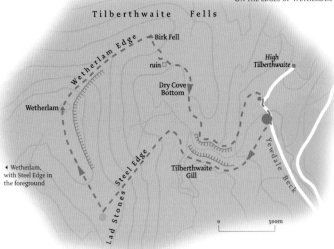

Tilberthwaite Fells

Wetherlam Edge · Birk Fell

ruin □

Dry Cove
Bottom

High
Tilberthwaite ▪

Wetherlam ▲

Steel Edge

Lad Stones

Tilberthwaite
Gill

Yewdale Beck

◄ Wetherlam,
with Steel Edge in
the foreground

0 _____ 500m

the jumble of crags and tilted boulders along Wetherlam Edge, keeping a northeast bearing. Gradually a worn line emerges, dropping out of the rock to a green saddle (Birk Fell Hawse), ahead of a small grassy top. Traverse ENE over the first top and then cut right through a trough before the second, joining a pitched path weaving southeast over steep ground. By the approach to a ruined working the gradient levels and the path widens to a quarry

track (2h30). Contour in an arc around the eastern rim of Dry Cove Basin, an inaccurately named, soggy bowl, with the massive bulk of the mountain hanging to the west.

Merge into a good path clinging above the sheer north wall of Tilberthwaite Gill, descending steadily to just above the row of quarrymen cottages. A lane cuts back in front of the houses to the road, and the car park is just beyond (3h15).

Quarrying

Man's principal contributions around and above Tilberthwaite are the many holes dotting the landscape. Quarrying for slate and copper was once big business here, and evidence of this is everywhere, lingering shadows of our predecessors' ingenuity and determination. The holes vary from the huge (up the road at Hodge Close) to the elegant (the complex of slate-lined hollows fringing the southern edge of Tilberthwaite Gill) and to the dank and sinister (Wetherlam, the bowl around Dry Cove Bottom and the area north towards Little Langdale are pitted by levels and shafts). Any explorations are a matter for individual judgement, though no one should go near the levels and shafts.

A very Victorian deception

Distance **9km** Time **2 hours 30**
Height gain **240m** Map **OS Explorer OL7**
Access **Coniston is served by the X12
from Ulverston and by the 505 from
Ambleside/Windermere (Stagecoach)**

**When James Garth Marshall decided that
his estate at Monk Coniston was
insufficiently picturesque, he planted an
exotic arboretum and set about
landscaping an idyllic tarn, Tarn Hows,
the fame (and popularity) of which
remains undimmed. The point of his
efforts may be debatable, but the charm
of this rolling excursion to his house and
tarn is indisputable.**

Start at the LDNPA car park in the centre
of Coniston. Walk east out of the village
by the B5285, picking up a footpath (safely
tucked a hedgerow's width away from the
road) just beyond the hump-backed
bridge over Yewdale Beck. Shadow the
road for just over 1km to a sharp left bend
by the head of Coniston Water. Cross to a
side road skirting the top of the lake (with
a great view down it), then turn through a
gate to the left after 250m (SP Tarn Hows

via Monk Coniston). A broad green way
makes a gentle ascent through parkland
to the collection of trees ringing Monk
Coniston House. Weave through the
arboretum (do inspect the elegant,
hexagonal gazebo there), then swing right
on a path cutting oddly through the
walled, and recently restored, kitchen
garden. Out the other end, trend left over
a track to join a terrace running NNE
through the specimen-dotted woods to a
hairpin bend on the B5285. Cross to the
equally lush woodland opposite.

A clear path (SP Permitted Path Tarn
Hows) ascends to cross a dammed beck
and then climbs a stone staircase to a
track. Bear right along this, back over the
beck and through mixed woodland. At a
T-junction with another track turn left,
before branching right 150m on (SP Tarn
Hows Old Car Park). Climb steadily, in the
latter stages alongside a wall, to a minor
road, where the Tarn Hows hollow is
suddenly revealed. Take the track
contouring opposite (towards Rose Castle),
cutting down after 400m to a slightly
dispiriting laid path encircling the tarn.

64

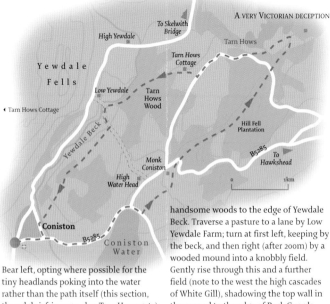

Bear left, opting where possible for the tiny headlands poking into the water rather than the path itself (this section, though brief, is as good as Tarn Hows gets).

From the tip of the tarn, head up the grassy bank to the road and turn right (1h30). Pass the National Trust car park and roll down the narrow road for 300m before turning right onto the tree-lined access track to whitewashed Tarn Hows Cottage. Enter the cottage yard and swing left to a gate into woodland, joining a meandering trail descending through handsome woods to the edge of Yewdale Beck. Traverse a pasture to a lane by Low Yewdale Farm; turn at first left, keeping by the beck, and then right (after 200m) by a wooded mound into a knobbly field. Gently rise through this and a further field (note to the west the high cascades of White Gill), shadowing the top wall in the second to the edge of Back Guards Plantation. Carry on in the same direction between pines, yews and gorse to open ground and a view over Coniston. Continue southwest, descending steadily, past the peculiar dog kennel folly (inscribed JGM 1855), to the edge of the town. Turn left along the road and then right at the T-junction with the B5285 to return to the centre of Coniston (2h30).

A study in the picturesque

Tarn Hows is self-consciously a 'beauty spot'. There were originally three small tarns, but Marshall dammed the lowest, landscaped the hollow and planted conifers to enhance and frame the views. This was the jewel of his 4000-acre estate and perfect for impressing visitors. In the 1920s the estate was split up and sold. Beatrix Potter snapped up the land (Tarn Hows included), sold on half to the National Trust at cost and then bequeathed the rest (1943). Two years later the Trust purchased the hall and gardens, completing the estate once again.

A hand on Dow Crag

▲ **Dow Crag** (778m)

Distance 9km Time 3 hours 30
Height gain 580m Map OS Explorer OL6
Access Coniston is served by the X12 from
Ulverston and by the 505 from
Ambleside/Windermere (Stagecoach)

Dow Crag, one of the great crags of the
Lakes, belongs to climbers. Or it usually
does, for amongst the ropes and the
belays and the talk of 'super severes',
there is a shallow gully that opens up the
forbidding east face to the walker. A head
for heights helps, but here with relative
ease is a thrilling chance to experience,
albeit fleetingly, the adrenaline rushes
and glamour of the mountaineer.

Start at the fell gate (the highest point
for cars) on Walna Scar Road, above
Coniston (GR289970). Walk WSW along
Walna Scar Road (now a stone track),
rising gradually to tiny Boo Tarn before a
brisk 600m stride on the level. As the track
ascends again it passes through two
distinct cuttings in the rock; 50m beyond

the second, branch right onto a good path
bearing northwest. Ascend steadily up the
southern flank of the Old Man to above
the basin known as 'The Cove', contouring
north with the deeply incised face of Dow
Crag now in sight ahead. Arc upwards
around the jutting Goat's Crag into the
hollow between the mountains, with
Goat's Water suddenly revealed as the
'corner' is turned. Few, if any, tarns in the
Lakes are more spectacular: a bowl of deep
blue wrapped tightly on three sides in
pink-grey rock.

Cross the outlet (GR266974) from the
tarn and clamber over the boulders at the
bottom of the slope. Traditionally, the
route to take up the scree led to the
stretcher box at the foot of the main
buttress, however, a more worn and
practicable line has developed south of
this (though it may still be heavy going),
heading up directly to the two deep
gullies set back on the left-hand side of
the face: Easy Gully (left, distinguished by
the finger of rock pointing upward just to

◀ Looking down the scramble route to Goat's Water

the left of its entrance) and Great Gully (right). Do not contemplate entering these and instead look left for a straight, scree-filled channel raking away from the base of Easy Gully. Though steep, the scramble up this channel is hugely entertaining with good rock to both sides and no particular difficulties. All that is needed is a clear head and confidence in using your hands.

Emerging on the grassy fell top, turn right and walk the short way north to the rocky summit of the crag (GR262977) (2h). Return south on a superb high-level traverse, weaving in line with the torn

edge of the crag tops, over the subsidiary tops of Buck Pike and Brown Pike (GR260966) – in between, note the pool of Blind Tarn wedged into the hillside far below. Off Brown Pike, drop steeply southwest to the saddle at Walna Scar Pass, turning down from here to the east. Back on the impossible-to-deviate-from Walna Scar Road, stick with it to the end, initially zigzagging steeply down (with Coniston Water ahead in the distance), then over more gently graded ground to Cove Bridge (1.5km on from the pass), and finally along the outward route, joined after a further 300m (3h30).

A Harry Griffin

A Harry Griffin OBE (1911-2004) is a genuine Lakes hero. Journalist, author and climber, Griffin dispatched terse and beautifully crafted columns for the Lancashire Evening Press *(and for The Guardian's 'Country Diary'), soaked in the rain running off the fells and rooted in the character of the communities in between. For over 50 years his elegant, vividly detailed prose lifted commuters from their trains and bored workers from their offices and transported them into the magic of the uplands. In his youth one of the 'Coniston Tigers' – a climbing group that pioneered routes all over the crags around the Old Man, Yewdale and, in particular, on Dow Crag – Griffin was out exploring the fells and writing about his experiences (including his fondness for discreet skinny dips in mountain tarns) well into his 80s.*

Coniston Water and Torver Common

Distance 8km **Time** 2 hours
Height gain 100m **Map** OS Explorer OL7
Access travel to Torver on the X12 from
Ulverston or Coniston

**There are all kinds of unexpected twists
and turns in wait around the Torver
Commons – from low rolling moorland
to the delightful higgledy shore of
Coniston Water.**

Start in the centre of Torver, at the
junction of the A593 and the A5084
(GR283941). Walk by the side of the A5084,
over the bridge and past the roadside
cottage, to a sharp right-hand bend. Bear
off to the left along a narrow metalled
lane, stick with it for 450m and then turn
right up the access track to
Brackenbarrrow Farm (SP To the Lake).
With the track, skirt the knot of farm
buildings, then fork right at its end onto
an enclosed path. Go through the first of a
pair of gates, along the foot of a wooded
slope and then through the second gate,
onto Torver Common. Descend a stony

path (keeping left – downwards – at the
fork) into woods, before levelling out and
crossing an open field to reach the side of
Coniston Water.

Turn right, heading south by the lake
shore, initially through a chilly conifer
plantation, then along an enjoyably rough
path haphazardly rising and falling on a
twisting line between the trunks and
knotted roots of native woodland. The
trees gradually thin and give way to gorse
and open ground, with the pebble shore
of the lake just below. Past Sunny Bank
Jetty follow the wall to climb away from
the water and curve, with a green track,
around to the small Torver Common
parking area, just off the A5084 (1h15).

Cross first the road to the footpath
opposite, then the footbridge over Torver
Beck and head up the valley. Around 200m
on from the beck, branch right on a path
weaving up between bracken around the
east slope of Anne Riggs. With the brown-
tinged wilderness of Torver Low Common
(in essence a low moor) revealed to the
west, drop down to join a track NNE
(GR282928) of a small reservoir.

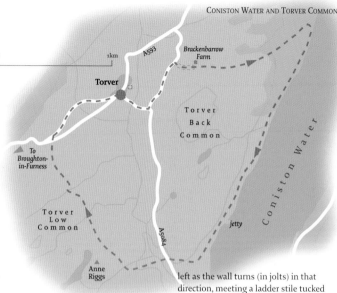

With the objective of meeting the intake wall to the northwest, set out over the common's seemingly endless humps and dips. First, cross the track and walk west to meet a more pronounced path and turn right. Keep right at a fork in the path just before a stream after 250m, soon enough drawing close to the intake wall. Ignore any inviting gateways and instead trend left as the wall turns (in jolts) in that direction, meeting a ladder stile tucked down to the right 150m on. Hop over this and negotiate a way (not hard) around copious gorse up to a gate in the top right corner of the field. Now bear straight (NNW) across a pair of fields, (the first, wavy one is a little reedy in its troughs) to emerge left of a house at a lane just off the A593. Drop down, cross the main road and follow the old one for a gentle, more-or-less traffic-free return into Torver (2h).

Donald Campbell

Reaching the lake shore, look over to the small island across the water. It was here, close to Fir Island, that Donald Campbell's final tilt at the water speed record came to an end on 4 January 1967. Travelling in Bluebird K7 at just over 300mph, the 45-year-old Campbell hit the wash from his just completed run down the lake. Captured on grainy black & white film, the vessel lifts, somersaults and hits the water with staggering force, killing Campbell instantly. A little of the British 'because it's there' tradition of cavalier derring-do also died that day.

◄ Sunny Bank Jetty

The Beacon and its Tarn

▲ Beacon Fell (255m)

Distance 6km **Time** 2 hours
Height gain 220m **Map** OS Explorer OL7
Access the X12 between Ulverston and
Coniston follows the A5084, with the
nearest formal stop at Blawith church,
a not very helpful 2km away

For a short expedition that is long on
character, say hello to Beacon Fell and
the tarn within its folds. Strangely, the
prominence of this small hill is out of
all proportion to its measly elevation;
perhaps that is the result of its setting,
sandwiched between a moorland
wilderness and the sheet of Coniston
Water. It does make for a great
viewpoint though.

Start at the most northerly of the
parking areas by Blawith Common, at the
edge of the A5084, just over 4km south of
Torver (GR286903). Walk north by the

roadside for 300m or so to a signed
footpath opposite Brown Howe Lodge.
Skirt a small marsh and rise to follow a
twisting path northwest through a
bracken-coated complex of mounds and
troughs. Arriving at a minor road, turn
uphill. After 600m, as the road executes a
first prominent right turn, break left by a
pair of holly trees on to a distinct path.
Pass beneath power lines and turn up
towards another holly tree on the incline
to the left. With the ridge of Beacon Fell
ever clearer to the south, dip through a
little valley and join the path ascending it,
emerging from a green rake between
tilted rock shelves to the cairned, heather-
fringed platform at the summit
(GR278906) (1h). Take your pick – there are
bleak views west, and watery ones east.

Traverse the fell top and head
southwest down the ridge to the northern
tip of Beacon Tarn. Follow the narrow

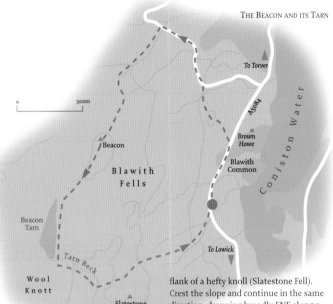

0   500m

Beacon

Brown
Howe

Blawith
Common

B l a w i t h
F e l l s

Coniston Water

A5084

Beacon
Tarn

Tarn Beck

To Lowick

W o o l
K n o t t

Slatestone
Fell

path (with encroaching gorse) along the length of the eastern edge of the water to the outlet at the southern end. Shadowing Tarn Beck, descend into a shallow basin richly decorated with bracken. Cross a wooden clapper bridge and fork left to slant upwards across the

flank of a hefty knoll (Slatestone Fell). Crest the slope and continue in the same direction, dropping broadly ENE along a weaving path back below the power lines and down towards Coniston Water. On reaching the A5084 bear left, either remaining by the roadside or, better, following the path from the parking area opposite down to the lake, then turning left after 350m to return to the start point (2h).

Swallows and Amazons for ever!

The southern end of Coniston Water lives in the popular imagination thanks to the children's classic Swallows and Amazons. *Arthur Ransome's novel captures the exploits of six children in the summer of 1929, sailing dinghies out to 'Wild Cat Island' (aka Peel Island) and engaging in all sorts of japes. As a child Ransome had regularly summered at High Nibthwaite, just off the bottom of the lake and the novel is suffused with local colour. Such was the success of its robust but idyllic portrait of childhood that Ransome spent the best part of the next 20 years turning out a series of follow-ups, of which four are also set in the Lakes.*

◀ Beacon Tarn from Beacon Fell

Wallowbarrow Crag and Gorge

▲ **Wallowbarrow Crag** (292m)

Distance 6km **Time** 2 hours 15
Height gain 240m **Map** OS Explorer OL6
Access do not rely on public transport as
a means of reaching the Duddon Valley.
The closest you will get is Broughton-in-
Furness, which is not close at all

Lurking deep within the otherwise sleepy
Duddon Valley, Wallowbarrow Gorge is a
spellbinding synthesis of wood, water
and rock. Combine the riverside traverse
through it with an ascent to the top of its
towering neighbour, Wallowbarrow Crag,
for a potent slice of the Lakes at their
most elemental.

Start by the roadside parking area just
west of Seathwaite, Duddon Valley
(GR224960). Walk towards the hamlet for
100m, turning left into the trees by the
second fingerpost. Cross a concrete
footbridge over Tarn Beck and follow the
water downstream to its confluence with
the River Duddon. Head upstream by the
river to just past a sharp bend to the right,
crossing the water either at stepping-
stones or at an elegantly arched stone
bridge 50m on.

Walk away from the water (pass left of
the solid rock dome) to a pasture,
crossing west to High Wallowbarrow
Farm. Join a bridleway leaving right of the
farmhouse and rise alongside Rake Beck
into woods. With an ever-developing
sense of the scale of the crag, ascend with
the tightly zigzagging path, across the
beck and clear of the trees, continuing up,
sandwiched between a wall and the crag,
to a level shoulder just short of a gateway.
Cut back at an angle up the coarse grass
slope to the right into a shallow combe
(this final ascent is an unexpected blend
of peat and heather). Take the channel
between low knolls, then branch right to a
rock tor with a further top beyond,
decorated with a rock finger
(GR222968)(45 minutes).

Return to the bridleway and go through
the gateway, immediately slanting right
on a track drifting gently upward to a
rounded moorland crest. Continue
through deer gates and traverse north

◀ The River Duddon rushing
through Wallowbarrow Gorge

Grassguards

River Duddon

To Wrynose
Pass

Grassguards
Native
Woodland

Wallowbarrow
Crag

Wallowbarrow
Gorge

Tarn Beck

High
Wallowbarrow

Seathwaite

To Ulpha

0   500m

across Grassguards Native Woodland, site of a Forestry Commission project to re-introduce juniper, rowan, oak and other species. Out of the enclosure, remain with the track through an impressively walled cutting and two further gates before descending slightly and resuming north. Use the permissive path rounding Grassguards Farm and cross the footbridge over Grassguards Gill. Head up the forestry track a few metres downstream, then split right after 25m on to a narrow path winding between trees, alongside the gill and just outside the boundary of the forest proper. Initially unpromising, the way gradually improves, particularly so in its final descent through the native wood by and beneath Fickle Crag (1h30).

Back alongside the Duddon, set off downstream. Whatever gentle image the words 'riverside walk' conjure in your mind will be swiftly dispelled by the next 1.5km, beginning with a sharp weave up a peaty bluff abutting the water. Drift gradually down the far side through fine woods and into Wallowbarrow Gorge, notable in the first instance for the scree sliding off the crag, high to the right. Stable, but bouldery, the route crosses the base of the scree to the most satisfying section of the walk: an engaging, thought-provoking and occasionally awkward

twist between massive boulders, trees and their roots, tucked beside the cascading river and deep within the gorge – glorious. Suddenly, beyond a wall, the terrain shifts back to woodland with only a short stroll back to the arched bridge crossed earlier. From here, reverse the outward route to return to the road (2h15).

Two Stickles and two Knotts

▲ **Hovel Knott** (220m), **Great Stickle**
(305m), **Stickle Pike** (375m),
The Knott (284m)

Distance **8km** Time **3 hours**
Height gain **450m** Map **OS Explorer OL7**
Access **Broughton-in-Furness has limited
public transport connections and is over
3km distant**

**A terrific network of neat, characterful
fells dot the upland between the Lickle
and the Duddon. Pre-eminent is Stickle
Pike, a rock-tipped pyramid possessing
the most perfect mountain profile in the
Lakes (even if, technically, it is only a
meagre hill). Pack your navigation skills
and prepare for the ups and downs of a
mini-adventure.**

Start by the telephone box in
Broughton Mills (GR222906). Walk north,
over the arched roadbridge over the River
Lickle, and rise northwest along a no-
through-road (ignore the two turnings
right) to its end by Green Bank Farm.
Branch right (SP Public Bridleway) and
pass left of a final whitewashed

cottage, joining a path weaving up at the
edge of a wood. Continue through the
gate at the far end into open country and
follow the obvious path curving ahead.
Slant left above the wall and make a
gentle upward traverse along a handsome
old green track, soon enclosed as a lane.
With a fine view ahead to the conical
Hovel Knott, cross a beck and remain with
the lane for 100m beyond a barn. Cut right
along a path aiming for the col right of
Hovel Knott, then break left at a suitable
point to make the short but entertaining
scramble to its compact top (GR211912).

Drop north into a trough then climb,
rounding right of a knoll, to rejoin the
main path. Gain the shoulder and swing
right (northeast), over a crest and across a
depression, to the trig-pointed summit of
Great Stickle (GR211916) (1h). Leave north
along the ridge, descending to the edge of
a large, marshy basin, aptly named Red
Moss. Cling to the foot of the slope
to the left to avoid this and then
go northwards.

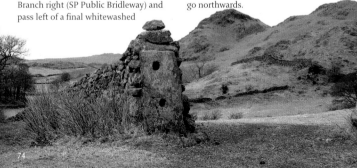

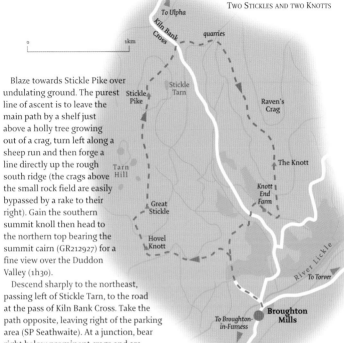

Blaze towards Stickle Pike over undulating ground. The purest line of ascent is to leave the main path by a shelf just above a holly tree growing out of a crag, turn left along a sheep run and then forge a line directly up the rough south ridge (the crags above the small rock field are easily bypassed by a rake to their right). Gain the southern summit knoll then head to the northern top bearing the summit cairn (GR212927) for a fine view over the Duddon Valley (1h30).

Descend sharply to the northeast, passing left of Stickle Tarn, to the road at the pass of Kiln Bank Cross. Take the path opposite, leaving right of the parking area (SP Seathwaite). At a junction, bear right below prominent crags and arc around a hollow to meet a bridleway left of a wall. Follow the bridleway SSE along the flank of the fell, drifting gently upward for 1km, eventually curving around to a saddle in the centre of the ridge. Leave the bridleway and bear south over a broad grassy rise to the nondescript top of The Knott (GR224919) (2h30). Continue south, dropping steeply to above the intake wall, where a terrace sweeps right to Knott End Farm. Walk through the farmyard and down the farm track beyond to the road.

Cross to the path opposite and drop to a delightful clapper bridge over Dunnerdale Beck. Ascend, passing through a gate (not into the wood) before curving right to join the track to Scrithwaite Farm. Follow this left, passing in front of the farmhouse, and then cut down to the left by a pine copse. Keep right of a wall leading back to the gate into the woods left at the beginning of the walk. Now retrace the way back to Broughton Mills (3h).

◀ Hovel Knott

75

Where the fells meet the sea

▲ **Black Combe** (600m)

Distance 8.5km **Time** 3 hours
Height gain 550m **Maps** OS Explorer OL7
Access to try and reach the start point
by public transport is futile – the car
rules here

The high ground makes a last hurrah
before the Irish Sea at the evocatively
named Black Combe, tucked into a corner
above the Duddon estuary and separated
from the murky waves by only a narrow
coastal corridor. Open and rounded, with
something of the flavour of Skiddaw or
the Howgills, it is the view (more than
the ground itself) that necessitates a
visit. So save Black Combe for a clear day,
when you may just be able to see forever.

Start at the lay-by off the A595 at
Beckside (GR152846), 3km west of the

junction with the A5093. Cross the road
and walk up the lane opposite. Pass a
scatter of buildings and skirt, in a wide
rising arc, around the tucked-down
Whicham Mill, remaining with the track
to its end at the fell gate. Strike out into
the 'V' of the narrow Whitecombe Valley,
along a good path rising gently alongside
Whitecombe Beck, with the screes of
Black Combe – the defining element in
the landscape – appearing as a huge
charcoal-green crescent across its head.

After a sheltered kilometre, cross a
bridge over the beck and climb a short
way before cutting sharply left to rake
upwards across the flank of White Combe,
with a fine close-up of Whitecombe
Screes. Follow the path along a wide
zigzag before levelling out and heading
north to the shoulder at Whitecombe
Head (1h15). Contour left around a vaguely
marshy area to gain the dull slope topping
the screes. Now head southwest for 2km

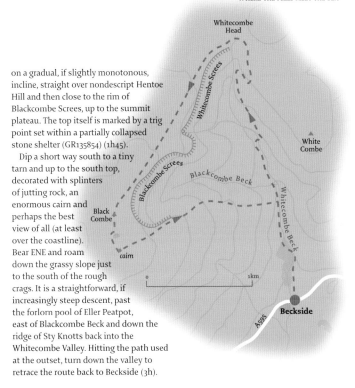

on a gradual, if slightly monotonous, incline, straight over nondescript Hentoe Hill and then close to the rim of Blackcombe Screes, up to the summit plateau. The top itself is marked by a trig point set within a partially collapsed stone shelter (GR135854) (1h45).

Dip a short way south to a tiny tarn and up to the south top, decorated with splinters of jutting rock, an enormous cairn and perhaps the best view of all (at least over the coastline). Bear ENE and roam down the grassy slope just to the south of the rough crags. It is a straightforward, if increasingly steep descent, past the forlorn pool of Eller Peatpot, east of Blackcombe Beck and down the ridge of Sty Knotts back into the Whitecombe Valley. Hitting the path used at the outset, turn down the valley to retrace the route back to Beckside (3h).

Infinite revelation

In the determinedly patriotic View from the Top of Black Comb (1813), Wordsworth states that from here, '. . . the amplest range/Of unobstructed prospect may be seen/That British ground commands'. Even if that overstates it, this is a unique view, overlooking the water to the other three countries of the United Kingdom: beyond a sharply etched Isle of Man to the distant heights of Northern Ireland and Wales, and across the Solway Firth to Scotland. Turning around, the view back to the northwest spans almost the full range of the Lake District fells. It is impressive. The great man nails it when he writes: 'In depth, in height, in circuit, how serene/The spectacle, how pure! – of Nature's works,/In earth, and air, and earth-embracing sea,/A revelation infinite it seems'.

◄ Friendly locals by Whicham Mill

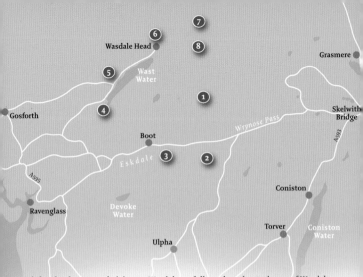

It is hard to be a casual visitor to Wasdale or Eskdale – the journey there is too long or too much of a struggle for it to be otherwise. If, somehow, you found yourself there without purpose, you would quickly find one, for these two valleys are a walker's dream. Largely straight, largely narrow and largely enclosed, one dominated by a lake and the other scratched by a river, they present an almost unarguable case for the beauty that arises when valley, mountain and water collide. So compact are they, and the detail so exquisite, there is only one real way to explore; you will have your boots on before you know it.

Wasdale splits into three: captivatingly beautiful Nether Wasdale could be an end in itself, but instead leans towards the promise of more; the dark waters of Wastwater (the deepest in England)

follow; then the starkness of Wasdale Head – a couple of farms, an inn, a tiny church and a ring of mountains (England's highest). This is a place of legends – of pioneer climbers, of evocatively named fells (Great Gable, Steeple), of hairs-breadth escapes and of tragedies. Pared back to these simplicities (and extremities), and with the spirit and the senses elevated, life seems more immediate in Wasdale. There is no better place.

Eskdale is softer and less obvious. Best known for the stream engine that nudges into one end of the valley and for the perils of Hardknott Pass at the other, the little ribbon of green in between is easily overlooked. The valley is a wonderful place, but above is even better, whether on your way to the lonely upper reaches or to the almost perfect Harter Fell.

78

ESKDALE, WASDALE AND THE MOUNTAINS

A glimpse into Upper Eskdale

▲ **Throstlehow Crag** (404m)

Distance 10.5km **Time** 3 hours 15
Height gain 340m **Maps** OS Explorer OL7
Access the only concession to public
transport in Eskdale is the steam railway,
which reaches as far as Dalegarth.

**There are two reasons to reach for the
unheralded heights of Upper Eskdale:
one, you seek an unfrequented route to a
summit upon the Scafell massif; or, two,
you wish to view close-up what is – bar
none – the most imposing scene in the
Lakes, the soaring semi-circle of
mountains from Sca Fell to Bowfell. With
a hint of wilderness – often pathless and
with an infant river to ford – Upper
Eskdale is an adventurer's delight.**

Start at the telephone box at the foot of
Hardknott Pass, Eskdale (GR211011). Walk
down the lane to Brotherilkeld Farm,
splitting left before the farmyard to a
fenced path along the east bank of the

River Esk. The way opens out onto a track
weaving up through a pair of rather soggy
fields before returning back towards the
water beyond the intake wall. With the 'V'
of the valley becoming increasingly
defined (and lined at its top by impressive
rock walls – Heron Crag to the west and
Yew Crag to the east), a good path sweeps
towards Lingcove Bridge with
Throstlehow Crag in view ahead.

Cross the delicate span of the bridge just
above the confluence of the Esk and
Lingcove Beck. Ascend right, between the
rock tower to the north (Throstle Garth)
and Lingcove Beck. As the gap between
the two narrows with height, the beck
drops into a ravine with some impressive
torrents. Beyond Throstle Garth,
Throstlehow Crag returns into view – head
north to a small craggy dome in front and
to the right of the main crag, so avoiding
the worst of a potentially damp slope.
Having gained slightly higher

ground, rise north to a tumbledown wall traversing the crag's east shoulder, swinging west up the sharpening slope to the summit (GR227043) (1h30). The views are magnificent, particularly to the cirque of mountains from the northwest to the northeast.

Roam north off the top towards the foot of Scar Lathing, a sheer rock pyramid looming above the river. Cross a tributary and, clinging to the base of the crag (any closer to the water is marshy), walk west, shadowing the river. Round a solid corner to the north, with the river now alongside, to the lip of Great Moss, a vast marshy plateau backed to the northwest by a massive cliff, Cam Spout Crag. Follow the river as it bends back to the left and look for a suitable place to cross – usually possible with dry feet by the next bend back to the right, though impossible anywhere if the river is in spate.

Climb to join a path contouring across the slope in a southern arc into the wide channel between Silverybield Crag and the line of crags running south from Green Crag. Continue into a basin, keeping along the higher ground by the western edge to skirt the dreadful marsh around Damas Dubs. The path leads over the beck, through a trough and begins to descend steeply, zigzagging down to the intake wall. Bear right, along a green track over Scale Bridge (notable for the view of Scale Gill's whitewater) and through a succession of pastures to a lane leading to Taw House. Enter the farmyard and turn immediately left along a permissive path to a footbridge over the river. Cross the bridge and turn right to return past Brotherilkeld Farm to the road (3h15).

◂ Lingcove Bridge

Classical Harter Fell

▲ **Harter Fell** (649m)

Distance 7.5km Time **3 hours 15**
Height gain 590m Maps **OS Explorer OL7**
Access buses are non-existent in Eskdale,
though the steam railway is a pleasant
way to get as far as Dalegarth

For the classic Eskdale ascent, look high
above Hardknott Pass to the soaring peak
of Harter Fell. Combine your trip with a
visit to the Roman remains of the
celebrated Hardknott Fort.

Start at the telephone box at the foot of
Hardknott Pass, Eskdale (GR211011). Walk
over the roadbridge and cattle grid, turning
down past the wood to cross Hardknott Gill
at Jubilee Bridge. Rise to a path first
traversing WSW along the base of the fell

before climbing beside the far wall. Ford
Dodknott Beck and pass through two gates,
300m apart, separated by a southwestern
rake. Beyond the second gate climb directly
up the slope, branching left after 100m for a
gentle grassy ascent towards the craggy
summit cone. Bear east along a clearly
defined route just to the right of the main
crags, weaving sharply up between heathery
tufts and broken rocks to a grassy channel
reaching up to the trio of rock towers at the
summit. The first to the left boasts a trig
point (GR218997), but the second, awkward,
top is marginally higher (although probably
only purists will care) (1h45).

Descend east, though a ring of tilted
rocks, to join a good path bearing
northeast. Skirt east of Demming Crag –

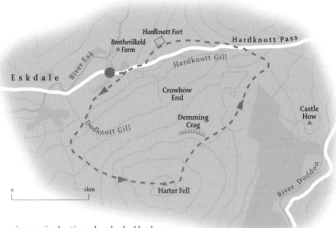

an impressive bastion when looked back on – and shadow a small ravine down. Round a marshy area to a fenced corner, high above the grim spectre of the conifers looming over the Duddon Valley that used to run to the fence (the upper swathe has been felled in the last few years). Cross the stile and negotiate another soggy patch, tracking the fence over a pair of knolls, then cross a stile to the right before a more prominent rise. Round to the right

of a rock corner, branching left before the next knoll to reach the road.

Head downhill, turning off to the right at the first sharp bend, roaming northwest to the Roman fort. Have an explore, and then pick up a path descending to the road before the next field wall. Continue down into the valley to the sounds of straining engines and burning brakes (3h15).

Hardknott Fort

Wandering down the road from the top of Hardknott Pass (bliss when winter forces its closure to vehicles), with Eskdale stretching out ahead and the Irish Sea disappearing into the distance, it is easy to imagine why the Romans chose this site as a stronghold. Mediobogdum (aka Hardknott Fort), a network of well preserved walls, remains defiant to this day, though now with only the weather (rather than the Scots) as its foe. Built between AD120 and 138, the fort was abandoned in the middle of the following century. It is thought that its garrison held around 500 men.

Eskdale water

Distance **8km** Time **2 hours 15**
Height gain **180m** Map **OS Explorer OL6**
Access **L'al Ratty** steams up from
Ravenglass and terminates at Dalegarth

**There may be no lake in Eskdale, but the
pull of water is as strong here as it is
anywhere in the south, from the
formidable gorge of Stanley Ghyll (the
Lakes' best) to the sweet waters of the
River Esk. Dip in.**

Start at Dalegarth Station, Eskdale
(GR173007). Walk west along the valley
road, turning left after 250m along a
narrow side road by the parish war
memorial. Descend with the lane to cross
a fine old roadbridge over the River Esk
then continue along to a fork before
Dalegarth Hall. Take the track to the left,
curving southeast to the edge of
woodland. Pass through a gate signed
'Waterfalls', walk ahead to Stanley Ghyll
and turn upstream into a spectacularly
green landscape of specimen trees,
rhododendron and – everywhere – moss.

Ascend alongside whitewater cascades,

the walls of the gorge becoming gradually
steeper and deeper. Three footbridges
carry the path back and forth over the
water; just beyond the highest of these
the path comes to a dead end at a narrow,
tilted and exposed shelf with a great, if
precarious, view to the main attraction:
the falls of Stanley Force and its plunge
pool. Return to the second bridge, but do
not cross; instead, follow a ramp left to a
stepped path cutting up the side of the
gorge beside a tributary. At a junction of
paths, bear left over the stream and zigzag
up between trees to a rock platform at the
top edge of the gorge. Believe the signs:
the terrifying drop off the platform is
sheer and deep.

Continue up, over a ladder stile, to
bracken-clad open fell. Slant right to a
green track, inclining left with this past a
small plantation to a whitewashed
cottage, Low Ground (GR174988). Join the
access lane beyond, turning left after
100m on the farm track to Whincop. Walk
through the farmyard, take a path leaving
left of the main house and descend north,

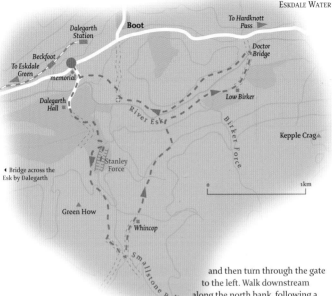

Boot

Dalegarth
Station

Beckfoot
To Eskdale
Green

memorial

Dalegarth
Hall

River Esk

To Hardknott
Pass

Doctor
Bridge

Low Birker

Kepple Crag

Birker Force

◀ Bridge across the
Esk by Dalegarth

0   1km

Stanley
Force

Green How

Whincop

Smallstone Beck

shadowing right of a wall to a ladder stile (1h). Beyond, trend right across saturated ground and over a ruined wall, continuing in the same direction to another collapsed wall traversing the slope below Hartley Crag. Follow this through bracken to its end (roughly 250m) and then drop a short way through trees to a squeeze stile. Descend sharply to the valley floor, joining the main path by a small conifer plantation.

Turn right (look for the tiny, reedy tarn within the ring of trees) and undulate past the bottom edge of native woodland to Low Birker. Swing down in front of the house and follow the access track back to the Esk, cross the arch of Doctor Bridge

and then turn through the gate to the left. Walk downstream along the north bank, following a roughly pitched path that moves away from the water into a walled section. From this a smooth green carpet (with a fine view across the valley to the falls at Birker Force) gives way to gorse and to a terrace back above the river. The path cuts straight at a meander then draws close to the water above a footbridge; descend to the wide riverside path by the bridge (but do not cross it). Continue by the north bank to Eskdale's humble, idyllically set church, St Catherine's.

Take the lane away from the river, branching left after 100m onto an initially walled path weaving back to the minor road left at the outset. Turn right to return to the valley road (2h15).

Above the intake to the lake

**Distance 7.5km Time 2 hours
Height gain 100m Map OS Explorer OL6
Access on Thursdays and at weekends
the 'Wasdale Taxibus' (no. 13) runs, if
pre-booked, to and from Whitehaven
and Seascale**

**The pastoral delights around Nether
Wasdale are at least three-fold: a glorious
and ancient patchwork of walls, woods
and fields, a sublime shoreline, and
officially (if you believe in these things),
'Britain's Best View'. There may be no
more beautiful walk in the Lakes.**

Start at Cinderdale Bridge, Nether
Wasdale (GR128038). Take the road in
the direction of Santon Bridge, cross Forest
Bridge and then turn off by the second
signpost to the left (SP Public Bridleway,
Eskdale). Walk along the left-hand edge of
two handsome fields, past tiny Flass Tarn,
to the corner of a conifer plantation.
Ascend inside the perimeter of the wood,
the key point being to remain alongside
the wall to the left, firstly at a meeting
with a forestry road and then at a fork.

Continue by the wall on a contour out of
the trees to a smooth green path.

Descend towards but not as far as
Easthwaite Farm, picking up a path
traversing to the intake wall as it rises
beyond the farm. Undulate upwards, by a
thin green ribbon through bracken, to the
shallow gully of Greathall Gill. Cross the
gill and weave beside the intake
wall – with a first view over Wastwater –
back to the valley floor.

Go through a pair of swing gates, first to
the left and then to the right, into a copse
bordering the River Irt. Follow the river
northwest for 300m to the elegant arch of
Lund Bridge (GR141039) (45 minutes). Cross,
passing through a five-bar gate and a swing
gate into Low Wood. Return southeast,
rejoining the banks of the Irt at a laid path.
Follow this around a small bay and
headland (with boathouse) to the tail of
the lake, wonderfully set beneath the
towering cliffs of Whin Rigg. Curve
along the glorious shoreline to open
ground, past stately Wasdale
Hall (now a youth hostel)

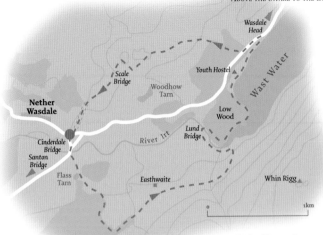

and through a rhododendron corridor to the end of the path at a rocky knoll.

Turn back along the road, over a cattle grid, to a wooded lane 250m further on. Turn up to the right, past the forlorn remains of a walled garden, staying with the ruler-straight lane to its end. Over a ladder stile, trend left to a green track meandering west through a rough and reedy, gorse-dotted pasture. Continue beyond the gate at the field end, then turn right after 150m (SP Buckbarrow), following an initially fenced section (note the grooves and notches in the stone gateposts to the left at its end). Slant left to a junction with an old cobbled bridleway (where the grass is now winning) and bear left, over the arch of Scale Bridge and into the field beyond. Shadow the wall to the left for 400 pastoral metres to Mill Place. Walk between the cottages, over the bridge and along the access lane back to Cinderdale Bridge (2h).

Going nuclear

Whatever the rights and wrongs of nuclear power, there can be no doubting the importance of the industry to the West Cumbrian economy. In an area heavily dependant upon public sector jobs, Sellafield directly employs 10,000 people. Today, the complex is primarily a waste management and reprocessing facility with, it is said, the two most hazardous industrial buildings in Europe: depositories of contaminated material from the early days of the nuclear industry (a lengthy and expensive clean-up operation is now under way). If it all feels a long way from the shore of Wastwater, bear in mind that Sellafield's owner, the NDA, extracts up to four million gallons of water a day from the lake.

◄ The view across Wastwater

A Middle way

▲ **Middle Fell** (582m)

Distance 6km **Time** 2 hours 30
Height gain 510m **Map** OS Explorer OL6
Access on Thursdays and at weekends
the 'Wasdale Taxibus' (no. 13) runs, if
pre-booked, to and from Whitehaven
and Seascale

A close neighbour of some of England's
highest and most evocative mountains,
and with an irretrievably bland name,
Middle Fell is easily overlooked. But this
comparatively modest hill above the west
shore of Wastwater has a secret – a
traverse of its knobbly and rugged slopes
is not only quick and easy, but also hugely
entertaining and a great alternative to the
familiar heights.

Start by the cluster of houses at
Greendale (GR144056), 750m southwest of
the road junction above the west shore of
Wastwater. Walk from the roadside east of
the cottages along a wide green path to
the right of Greendale Gill. Ascend steeply
north, ignore the path descending from
the right (to be used later) and follow the
beck into a sheltered gully. Rise on a
winding, generally stony line sandwiched
between the rough white bed of the gill
and the bracken-covered side of the gully.

With a slackening gradient, cross a
marshy area to reach the southern tip of
Greendale Tarn (45 minutes), a placid
sheet of water tucked beneath the hostile
western flank of Middle Fell. Round the
eastern edge of the tarn on a narrow path,
negotiating a rocky area in the process,
and then forge a line north up a coarse,
boulder-scattered grass slope to a
windswept plateau in the saddle between

Seatallan and Middle Fell.

From the saddle, bear southeast, picking up a faint path and passing left of a clefted rock tower. Drift around to the south on a gradual upward trajectory over increasingly craggy and broken ground before rising more purposefully to a depression. The summit cairn (GR150072) (1h30) is set upon the rock shelf at its far end – a wonderful, and little known place from which to view The Screes and the Scafell massif.

Descend southwest, sidestepping the numerous low crags punctuating the rough grass slope. There is no particular path – just keep your bearing and choose the branches and channels between the crags that most appeal. With a steepening of the slope, a more distinct line develops, moving around to above the gully and down to the junction of paths passed at the outset. Finish the descent by the outward route, returning through the lush, pea-green pastures of Greendale to the road (2h30).

Joss Naylor

Wasdale farmer Joss Naylor MBE is perhaps Britain's greatest fell runner, and certainly the most celebrated. His achievements are legion: in 1975, he capped a series of endurance records by making a circuit of 72 Lakes peaks – covering over 100 miles and ascending 38,000ft – in only 23 hours and 20 minutes. As if to prove that he could still cut it at the age of 70, in 2006 he ran to more than 70 Lakes tops – on a route extending over 50 miles and rising 25,000ft – in a remarkable 21 hours. That all rather sets a walk up Middle Fell in context.

◀ Middle Fell from the shore of Wastwater

The Y of Mosedale

Distance 4.5km **Time** 1 hour 15
Height gain 100m **Map** OS Explorer OL6
Access on Thursdays and at weekends
the 'Wasdale Taxibus' (no. 13) runs, if
pre-booked, to and from Whitehaven
and Seascale

If a narrow valley and high mountains
define Wasdale, nowhere is the contrast
better expressed than in its tiny offshoot
Mosedale, wrapped within a ring of
soaring rock. A circle of the valley –
notable for a charming waterfall and
curious boulder – is perfect for when
time is tight, the heights have been
conquered, or when the sun is setting.

Start at Wasdale Head village green
(GR187085). Walk to the Wasdale Head Inn,
turn down the lane past Ritson's Bar and
cross the old packhorse bridge over

Mosedale Beck. Bear right, rising through
an enclosed lane and the field beyond, to
the top edge of a larch copse. Cut down
through the second gap in the wall (the
first is soggy), descend between the trees
and move slightly downstream to view
Ritson's Force, a handsome waterfall,
magical in dappled sunlight. Continue
upstream by the water, rejoining the main
path by the end wall.

Through a gate, and, with the towering
arc of the Mosedale mountains ahead,
follow the path around a knoll and ford a
shallow tributary. Skirting the damp,
mossy valley bottom, cross a field
decorated with scattered boulders
(resembling standing stones) to a lovely
sheepfold built around two of these.

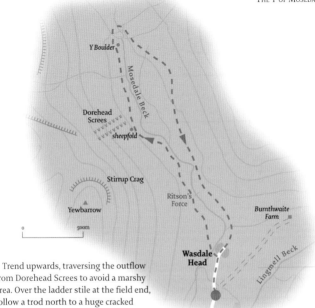

Trend upwards, traversing the outflow from Dorehead Screes to avoid a marshy area. Over the ladder stile at the field end, follow a trod north to a huge cracked stone, the 'Y' Boulder (GR178104), named for the shape of its fissures. Cross the tiny stream to the right of the boulder and head upstream to locate an easier place to ford stony Mosedale Beck.

Returning downstream, cross three minor tributaries by their confluence, and then slant left to a gate by sheepfolds. An easy contour SSE leads quickly to the bridleway descending from Black Sail Pass. Sweep back down the valley, rising to a gate above a wall. Shadow left of the wall on an elevated line, descending to a further gate. Through this, fork right, rejoining Mosedale Beck for the short walk back into Wasdale Head (1h15).

The birthplace of British climbing

Ritson's Force is named after Will Ritson (1808-90), the legendary founder and proprietor of the Wastwater Hotel (now the Wasdale Head Inn). In 1856, Ritson converted a farmhouse to accommodate overnight guests, and a base for the emerging British climbing scene was born. The Victorian era was a golden age for Wasdale Head, with climbing pioneers such as W P Haskett Smith, Owen Glynne Jones and Cecil Slingsby all forging new routes on the crags of Great Gable and Scafell.

Looping Great Gable

Distance **6km** Time **4 hours 30**
Height gain **720m** Map **OS Explorer OL 6**
Access **on Thursdays and at weekends
the 'Wasdale Taxibus' (no. 13) runs, if
pre-booked, to and from Whitehaven
and Seascale**

**Why is it that mountains are always
considered places you should get to the
top of? When it comes to Great Gable,
savvy walkers know that the majestic
South and North Traverses, exhilarating
and inspiring paths forged by the Victorian
pioneers of rock climbing, are the best
routes on the mountain. Find them linked
here on this thrilling round.**

Start at Wasdale Head village green
(GR187085). Walk north by the farm track,
past tiny yew-ringed St Olaf's Church and
between stone-cleared pastures to
Burnthwaite Farm. Round to the left of the
farmhouse on to Moses' Trod, a rough
stone track. Beyond the footbridge over
Gable Beck, slant upwards to a gate.

Rise steadily along a well-worn path, over
stable scree, onto pitches and then to the
pass at Sty Head, distinguished by its
landmark stretcher box (GR218095) (1h).

Two paths bearing west leave just to the
Wasdale side of the box; take the one to the
left – a fainter line traversing between grass
mounds – the beginning of the South
Traverse. Becoming rockier, the trail leads
to the base of the cracked walls of a vast
bastion, Kern Knotts. Scramble over the
large boulders at the foot of the main
buttress, then, hugging the base of smaller
crags, cross a hollow to a small cave with
trickling water. Make the short scramble
from here to gain a line across some scree
and over the top of a gully. Contour easily
to a larger gully, the red-tinted Great Hell
Gate, raking across this and around a low
buttress. Amid the distinctly rockier
ground beneath the Great Napes, the finger

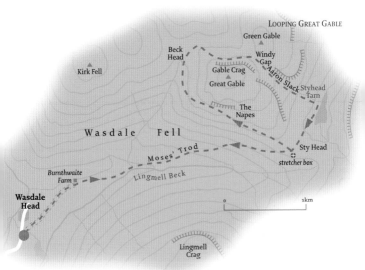

of Napes Needle is visible above. An awkward return scramble to the base of the needle may be made from here, but if you wish to take a closer look it is better to make the detour via the next red scree-shoot, the narrow and steep-sided Needle Gully. Otherwise, stick with the path as it twists around rock protrusions, but look to cut down before the final gully, the misleadingly named Little Hell Gate, there being a troublesome set of rock steps to it off the end of the 'main' route (2h).

Continue past Little Hell Gate to the tip of the distinct corner where the southern and western flanks meet, contouring north over the extended rock field beyond. Hold the line over rock-broken grass to the peaty fringe before Beck Head, taking the clear path inclining right. Merge into the eroded path weaving up the northwest ridge and gain around 50m in height; at 730m look for

two small cairns perched left of the path, the door to the North Traverse. Little more than a thin ribbon, the traverse gently undulates beneath the length of the formidable wall of Gable Crag. Past a dip at the end, curve up along a rock run (well to the south of the obvious path rising from Moses' Trod) to the saddle at Windy Gap (3h). Crest and descend by Aaron Slack, on a direct line to the blue pool of Styhead Tarn, over a blend of scree (upper stages) and pitches (lower reaches) and, for the most part, following the beck.

At the main path by the side of Styhead Tarn bear south, up the grassy bank, to the top of the pass. Say hello to the stretcher box again (so completing the loop) and pick up the outward path back to Wasdale Head, enticed forward along the hour-long return by the promises of refreshment in the valley below (4h30).

◀ The southern face of Great Gable

Along the edges of Piers Gill

▲ **Lingmell** (807m)

Distance 9.5km **Time 4 hours 15**
Height gain 730m **Map OS Explorer OL 6**
**Access on Thursdays and at weekends
the 'Wasdale Taxibus' (no. 13) runs, if
pre-booked, to and from Whitehaven
and Seascale**

**With its cascades of water and rock, the
ascent to Lingmell alongside Piers Gill
is the most spectacular ascent from
Wasdale Head.**

Start at Wasdale Head village green
(GR187085). Walk north by the farm track,
past tiny yew-ringed St Olaf's Church and
between stone-cleared pastures to
Burnthwaite Farm. Go round to the left of
the farmhouse to join Moses' Trod, a
rough stone track. Beyond the footbridge
over Gable Beck, branch right to join
Lingmell Beck as the wall beside it ends.

After 600m, just past the confluence
with Piers Gill, ford the rocky beck to a

defined path weaving through a series of
zigzags. At the head of a small knoll, break
off the path and ascend sharply up the
roughly grassed, rock-scattered slope to
the south. Gradually, a faint trod emerges
leading left of Piers Gill to a stream tucked
into a small ravine (GR214087). Cross this
(1h30) and swing southwest by a path
along the top edge of the gill, rewarded by
a first glimpse of the developing chasm.

As a bank of low crags cuts across the
path, scramble (trending right) to the top,
then take the thin channel rising beyond
(above a tiny subsidiary ravine) to open
ground. Return towards the gill edge (how
close is a matter for personal judgement –
the walls are dangerously sheer and deep),
remaining in line with it to the corner
where the gill bends back to the south.
The architecture of the omnipresent rock –
both down into the gill and up to Lingmell
Crag – is at its most powerful and
muscular here.

With the gradient slackening, it is a
surprisingly easy walk SSE up to and
across a shallow bowl to meet the top of
the well-worn Corridor Route (rising from

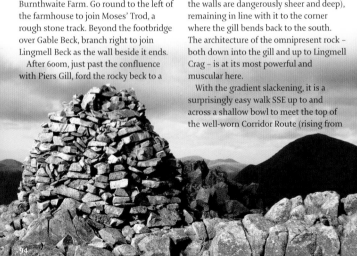

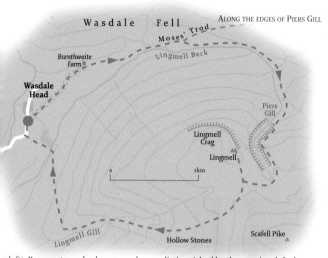

distinguished by the massive clefted crags of Sca Fell to the south – steepens into a pitched section descending Brown Tongue. As the gradient eases, ford right over Lingmell Gill (not to be confused with Lingmell Beck), pass through a gate and then fork right onto a thin path contouring around the nose of the ridge. With the hamlet in view ahead, rake down the slope (by a twisty path) to a footbridge over Lingmell Beck. Traverse west over a gorse-dotted field to the road, where it is a short way back to the simple but unbeatable charms of Wasdale Head (4h15).

e left). Bear west over broken ground
d stepped crags above the head of Piers
ll (which here only hints at the tumult
wnstream). After 200m, slant right over
ugh grass and the remains of a wall to
e saddle at Lingmell Col. A distinct route
ns NNW to the fine rocky summit,
pped by an elegant cairn resembling an
verted pinecone (GR209082) (2h45).
Return to just above the col and bear
utheast, back over the wall and across a
indswept plateau, to join the main path
scending from the col. An initially easy,
gzag descent through Hollow Stones –

e Sty Head road

*seems laughable now, but in 1897 plans were drawn up to build a road over Styhead Pass, so as to provide
 easy means of communication between Borrowdale and Wasdale'. The proposal was heartily supported
 the chairman of Keswick Urban District Council and by Mr J Musgrave, owner of Wasdale Hall, who
erred to the project as 'an admirable way of commemorating the Queen's extraordinary reign'. The idea
s sufficiently advanced for Cumberland County Council to have promised to cover half of the £10,000
st. Thankfully, the hare-brained scheme was soon to come to a dead end.*

ingmell's summit cairn

Index